Christianity
without **God**

Lloyd Geering

Christianity without
God

Polebridge Press

Christianity without God

Published in 2002 by Polebridge Press, P. O. Box 6144, Santa Rosa, California, 95406.

Library of Congress Cataloging-in-Publication Data

Geering, Lloyd George.
    Christianity without God / Lloyd Geering
        p. cm.
    Includes bibliographical references and index.
    ISBN 0-944344-92-5
    1. Death of God theology. I. Title

BT83.5 .G44 2002
230'.046--dc21   2002074987

To the treasured memory of
Elaine Geering
(1927-2001)
my beloved wife and loving
companion of nearly fifty years
(20 November 1951 – August 2001)
who died suddenly while this
book was being written.

Contents

Foreword

Christians have become a-theists. Translated into the common tongue: Christians are no longer theists. They no longer believe in a personal, objective, thinking God 'out there' somewhere. The theistic notion of God has not survived the acids of modernity. What then is the future of Christianity? Is Christianity tied irretrievably to a traditional doctrine of God?

In his inimitable way, Lloyd Geering has reframed this question as a thesis: Christianity should learn to exist without God. He believes we must take leave of God, if we are to refurbish Christianity with terms and incentives suitable to the global age we are now entering.

By taking leave of God, Christianity will continue on the early path it developed in the doctrine of the Trinity. In that doctrine, God was being humanized, and humankind, together with all creation, were divinized. God and world were being rejoined as in primitive nature religions. But the church intervened on behalf of a father deity and a patriarchal hierarchy. The result was an absolute monarchy dominated by men. By leaving God behind, we may hope to recover total human freedom, along with the affirmation of basic human rights. This move entails the abolition of slavery, the emancipation of women, and the acceptance of homosexuality. And, one might add, that move will do away with original sin and the stigmatization of sex. In addition, by forsaking the creation story in Genesis, it will restore respect for all of nature, thus enabling humankind to live in harmony with planet earth rather than raping nature for its own pleasure.

Lloyd Geering has produced a stunning, provocative, panoramic view of the evolution of Christianity in this new book. Christianity has reached the stage at which it must learn to exist without God — without an external authority figure who blesses and condemns arbitrarily. In place of that deity, he challenges us to assume responsibility for ourselves and for the earth we have inherited.

Robert W. Funk
Director, Westar Institute

Chapter One

An absurd question?

ould Christianity continue to exist without belief in God? At first it appears absurd even to pose the question. To most people, whether they regard themselves as Christian or not, it may seem self-evident that belief in God is the foundation stone on which Christianity is built. After all, do not the standard Christian Creeds actually begin with the words 'I believe in God...'?

Some people go even further and regard belief in God as the *sine qua non* of all religion. Such a limited view overlooks the fact that the Buddhist tradition dispensed with the belief in God (or gods) at the time of its origin. Yet Buddhism is regarded as one of the major religions of the world. It is even older than Christianity and has existed all this time without belief in any God. So it is possible for **religion** to exist without belief in God. But is it possible for **Christianity** to exist without belief in God?

Before we can adequately answer that question we must ask two other questions: What do we mean by Christianity? and What do we mean by God? In the course of this book we shall examine both of these questions at some length. If, in the course of that enquiry, we find it is not absurd but in fact quite possible to conceive of Christianity existing without belief in God (as traditionally understood), we can then proceed to explore what such a Christianity could be like.

1

Most people in the Western world, whether or not they still choose to identify with the Christian way of life, assume that when they use the words 'Christianity' and 'God', they have a pretty clear idea of what they are talking about. This is because Western culture has for many centuries been shaped by the Christian tradition and all Westerners have been more deeply influenced by it than they usually realize. In the Western world even atheists can be legitimately termed 'Christian atheists', since it is the idea of God traditionally held by Christians which they wish to reject.

As the official creeds bear witness, it is certainly true that in the past some kind of belief in God has played a very important role in Christianity. But when we come to examine the evolution of Western culture in general, and the long history of Christianity in particular, we very soon discover that clear and straightforward definitions for such terms as 'Christianity' and 'God' are hard to find. To make matters even more difficult, even those who think of themselves as Christians do not agree on what it means to be a Christian. At the beginning of the twentieth century, most people in the Western world would have been offended if you had suggested to them that they were **not** Christian. Today, some people in the churches are embarrassed if you ask if they **are** Christian, because in some quarters the term has been taken over almost exclusively by extreme evangelicalism and fundamentalism.

The problem of meaning has become so acute in connection with the term 'God' that it is now common in certain contexts to reflect this by writing the word in inverted commas. If it has become so difficult to define both Christianity and God, how can we be so sure that Christianity cannot exist without God? Even if the term 'God' were still deemed to be essential to Christianity, one must ask which particular meaning is intended.

It is true that in the past this confusion did not exist to the degree that it does today. (We shall be discussing in due course the various factors which have led to this cultural confusion.) At any particular time in the past, particularly after the fifth century, the Christian culture which began to spread over Europe was reasonably homogeneous (partly because those who did not agree with official doctrine were excommunicated). The reality of God was accepted without question as the foundation of Christianity; this belief was regarded as religiously and intellectually superior to the plurality of gods worshipped by the indigenous peoples. The meaning of the word 'God', as taught by Christians, seemed reasonably clear. That is why, when people in modern times found they could 'no longer believe in God' (as they said) they assumed it meant abandoning Christianity also.

This situation is now changing. Western culture is no longer as homogeneous as it was in the past. It is no longer wholly clear (as we shall presently see) what constitutes Christianity and whether or not it is permanently tied to one particular understanding of the word 'God'. An increasing number of people who no longer find the traditional idea of God convincing nonetheless wish to call themselves Christians in the sense that they wish to identify with most of the Christian values and ideas.

Some of these even want to continue serving in the role of ordained ministers, but have soon found themselves in conflict with church authorities. That was only to be expected. All new ideas or insights tend to be flatly rejected at first. At the present time, church authorities are still generally agreed that it is not possible to be a Christian minister or priest while at the same time questioning the traditional understanding of God. In recent years an Anglican clergyman was removed from his ministerial post because he appeared to his superiors no longer to believe in God in the way he was expected to.[1] This was in spite of the fact that that this scholarly and devout man was keen to remain within the ecclesiastical institution and to exercise a ministry within it.

The questions about Christianity and God which we are about to explore are of course very serious ones. They are often discussed in academic circles in highly technical and philosophical language which is far from clear to most lay people. I am going to discuss these serious issues, not only in very simple language but also, on occasion, in a more light-hearted way. This is to try to demonstrate the fact that we should not take theological statements too seriously.

The word 'theology' (as its Greek etymology shows) literally means 'talk about God'. What we are now coming to realize is that no talk — whether it is about God, or humankind, or the earth — can ever be anything other than human talk. When we talk about God we are using concepts and language which we humans,

3

as a species, have created over a long period of time. Even the word 'God' is a human creation[2], as is the English language as a whole; that is the reason why 'God' has to be translated by other words in other languages. When Christian missionaries took Christianity to China, they discovered to their surprise that there was no word in Chinese equivalent to 'God'. They had to invent one. What they actually did was to choose what they thought was the most suitable Chinese word and attempt to give it a new meaning. Unfortunately the Catholics chose one word and the Protestants chose another!

This story should bring home to us the fact that all of our ideas or concepts were 'invented' at some time in the past by humans. Thus the word 'God' is a human invention we have inherited from the past, however important we still regard the word to be. The human origin of all of our languages is something we humans have become aware of only in the last one hundred and fifty years. Up until the middle of the nineteenth century it seemed self-evident to our European ancestors (largely as a result of reading the opening chapters of the Bible) that human language existed from the creation of Adam and Eve, some six thousand years ago. And how did they learn it? Since these supposed first humans were described as being fully adult when they were created, it was natural for Bible readers to assume (if they thought about the question at all!) that they were already language speakers from the moment they were created. In other words language was just as much a part of the human condition as were their tongues and their brains. Indeed, a literal reading of Genesis 1 implies not only that language was divine in origin but also that it existed before the creation of the world, for the Bible explains how everything was created by the uttering of such words as, 'Let there be light' — whereupon there was light!

The ancient storytellers saw nothing odd in attributing creation to the utterance of words. Language fascinated the ancient mind. Although words could be heard they could never be seen or touched; yet the uttering of them seemed to be very powerful. A person of authority had only to say the right words and people obeyed. That is why the Israelite prophet could describe God as saying,

So shall my word be that goes forth from my mouth;
it shall not return to me empty,
but it shall accomplish that which I purpose,
and prosper in the thing for which I sent it.[3]

Belief in the power of language was the foundation on which rested the efficacy of blessings, curses, and incantations as practised in the ancient world (and almost up to the present). The nearly blind Isaac, having been tricked into blessing the wrong son, could not reverse what he had done; such was the power of the words he had uttered.[4] Prohibition of the blasphemous utterance of the Holy name of God (YHWH) became one of the Ten Commandments. From the fourth century B.C.E. onwards Jews took it so seriously that they soon forgot how the word had been originally pronounced, since the written form of the word did not contain the vowels.

In the biblical tradition, therefore, language with its mysterious power was thought to go back to the origin of the universe. Adam and Eve were already speaking it when they were created and they were able to converse with their Creator. Ancient scholars sometimes speculated as to what this original language was, and some contended it must have been Hebrew, that being the language in which the books of Moses were written.

According to the story of the Tower of Babel[5], all humans spoke this same proto-language until the time when, as an act of divine punishment for their hubris, they were driven to confusion when they found themselves speaking many different languages. The story implies that God had created these languages also, and then miraculously forced human tongues to speak them. (A similar view lies behind the phenomenon of glossolalia, or speaking in tongues, found in charismatic churches to this day).

The ancient biblical stories of the Garden of Eden and the Tower of Babel may seem quaint today. They even tell of God taking his 'constitutional' in the Garden of Eden in the cool of the day.[6] The stories soon lead to absurdity if we take them literally. For example, how could there be three days and nights before the sun was created on the fourth day? Where did Cain's wife come from? How could Cain build a city at a time when there existed only three people? And where did his son Enoch get his wife from?

Yet until 150 years ago these early stories of the Bible all seemed to be very convincing to our forbears and few people ever asked awkward questions about their logic.

In modern times, though only in the last century or so, we have been introduced to a very different account of human origins in general, and of the development of human language in particular. Such modern sciences as geology, zoology, anthropology, palaeontology, and ethnology have made us aware that life on this planet has existed for a very much longer period than previously thought. It was over that vast span of time that the many different species slowly and by subtle little changes developed into what they eventually became rather than being created all at once in their final form. This complex and exceedingly slow process of the diversification of life forms, including humankind, we refer to as the evolution of life on earth.

It is not at all surprising that of all the new ideas, philosophies, and technologies which have emerged in the last two hundred years, the notion of biological evolution is the one which has initiated most debate among Christians. Conservative Christians are still strongly opposed to it, and for understandable, even if indefensible, reasons. It is much more corrosive of traditional Christian beliefs than is often realized.

First, it completely contradicts the opening chapters of Genesis and provides an entirely different account of the origin of life on this planet, including that of the human species. It raises very serious questions about the process of creation itself. It renders unnecessary the postulation of a divine Creator for the creator's job was made redundant. For similar reasons Laplace (1749–1827) made his famous reply to Napoleon when the latter asked the celebrated astronomer where God fitted into his theory of the heavenly bodies: 'I have no need of that hypothesis'. All that has been very threatening to Christian orthodoxy; it gave rise within Christian circles to fierce theological debates which have never been wholly resolved.

Moreover, the idea of biological evolution led in turn to an evolutionary understanding of human culture. By human culture we mean the language, ideas, concepts, stories, rituals, moral codes, and religions which together constitute the way we understand the world in which we live. There are many cultures; each has its own unique character and formulates its own particular answer to the meaning of human existence. The diversity and impermanence of human cultures compel us to recognize that they have all slowly evolved from the very simplest of beginnings. Thus human cultures have been created or invented by humans over a very long period. Cultural evolution is still going on. We are adding to our own culture and changing it every time we come out with a new idea, coin a new term, replace one social practice with another, and develop a new philosophy or religion.

The replacement of the biblical description of origins by the evolutionary account has thus had the effect of radically changing our understanding of the real world. What even our quite recent ancestors believed to have come from an authoritative non-human source in the distant past now turns out to have been slowly and collectively created by our more distant ancestors, even though they were mostly unaware that they were creating anything. All languages, cultures, and religions have been humanly created.

Thus even more shocking to the traditional Christian than the story of biological evolution is that of cultural evolution. It shows us that all religious concepts and theological doctrines are human creations. All religious words, ideas, and teachings, which we have inherited from the past, were at some time created or formulated by humans. (Just how this happened with the concept of God we shall take up in chapter 3.)

Acknowledging that the language and words with which we express our beliefs have been humanly invented still leaves us free, of course, to discuss and debate the extent to which those concepts, ideas, and doctrines have for us 'the ring of truth' in describing the nature of reality. For to be believed, such concepts and doctrines must be able to win our conviction by their own inherent meaning. They can no longer be defended on the grounds that they go back to the beginning of the universe or have been revealed by some supernatural source.

All this places us in a very different situation from that in which our ancestors lived until quite recent times. It is as if our understanding of the real world has been turned inside out. The Christian culture which pervaded Europe for more than a thousand years looked at the world, as it were, from **inside** the Bible. Our forbears viewed reality through biblical spectacles; how they saw the world was in part determined by what was in the Bible. Indeed, when they drew their maps of the world, they placed the holy city of Jerusalem at the center. Because of the transition to modernity, things are now the other way round; we look at the Bible from the world **outside** of it.

It was long assumed in the Christian tradition (and strongly argued if that was thought necessary) that all the basic truths about reality had been divinely revealed in the distant past; it was a heinous sin even to question them. It was similar in the Islamic world, where the Qur'an, and not the Bible, was thought to be the depository of divine and infallible truth. Muslims believed (and still do) that the Qur'an was supernaturally revealed to Muhammad through the angel Gabriel and is therefore to be accepted without question.

Although the Bible itself attributes its various books to such people as Moses, Israelite prophets, Paul, and the Apostles, it came to be believed that these people had written under the direct guidance and inspiration of God. It was not really **their** thoughts they were writing down but the thoughts of the Almighty — as if they were no more than his hired stenographers. Thus through the centuries Christians came increasingly to view the Bible as the depository of divinely revealed knowledge in much the same way as the Muslim believes the Qur'an came directly from Allah. Some even referred to the Bible as the Word of God in written form. The Bible was judged to be wholly true and could not possibly contain error.

This view of the Bible became especially dominant in Protestantism, partly due to the power it placed in the hands of the Protestant Reformers. They were able to appeal to what they took to be the divine authority of the Bible in order to subject current church life and practice to criticism. In Catholicism, by contrast, the hierarchy had always retained the authoritative right to interpret the Bible in the light of ongoing tradition; thus the correct understanding was subject to change even though development was slow. That is why, at the Reformation, Catholics believed that making the Bible available to otherwise ignorant and unskilled readers was a very dangerous thing to do. The subsequent rise of many biblically based sects, each following its own preferred interpretation, has demonstrated the validity of their apprehension.

When Protestants appealed to the Bible in order to subject church tradition to criticism, it had the effect of raising the status of the Bible even further. This is illustrated by the fact that in the Reformed Confessions of Faith, trust in the Bible became the first Article.[7] Because the knowledge of God, including his will for the church, had now become dependent on the authority of the Bible, it was logical to leave the discussion of God to the Second Article. Few seem to have noticed that this had the effect of demoting God, in a way that the Creeds had never done. In the case of more extreme Protestants this meant that it was the Bible even more than God that they were worshipping. This state of affairs has been called bibliolatry.

The Protestant emphasis on the Bible found its extreme form in fundamentalism. It is one of the reasons why fundamentalists appear to be so confident and dogmatic, sometimes to the point of arrogance. Possessing the words of God in written form (as they believe they do) they know with great exactness just what God wills them to do and believe. Fundamentalists remind one of something once said by the ancient Arian Bishop Eunomius (died c. 395 C.E.) — "I know God as well as he knows himself!" In one sense this claim is quite laughable and megalomaniac. In another sense it is ironically true; for what fundamentalists believe to be the mind of God turns out to be what they have in their own minds (derived partly from reading the Bible and partly by interpreting the Bible in the light of their own experience and natural inclinations).

This trend of forcing the Bible to perform a role it is not capable of fulfilling was bound to end in disaster. The Bible was being turned into an idol. It was being used to lend its authority to whatever the reader (unconsciously) wished to believe or to do. Today the Bible has fallen from the pedestal on which Christian tradition had come to place it. Ironically, according to the Bible itself, that is just what should happen to idols.[8] It has taken a long time for the Christian community as a whole to accept what has happened to the Bible, and while fundamentalists still make the inerrancy of the Bible the foundation of their beliefs, even more liberal Christians still tend to depend ultimately on the Bible in making final pronouncements on matters of doctrine and ethics.

The changed status of the Bible does not at all mean that

it is no longer important. It retains a most honorable place among the holy writings of the world. It is a most valuable historical and religious resource. It is our chief historical witness to the origins of the Judeo-Christian tradition. What the Bible does **not** do, however, is to provide for all time an authoritative account of what humans should believe and do. In particular, the Bible does not provide tangible evidence of the existence of God, or infallible knowledge about the divine nature and will. The Bible has always been, and still remains, a set of human documents; it was written by humans and reflects the limited knowledge, as well as the common assumptions and prejudices, of the cultural contexts in which its various books were written.

The fall of the Bible from its pedestal occurred chiefly and most dramatically in the nineteenth century. As noted above, it was Charles Darwin's theory of biological evolution which brought the issue sharply to a head, since it directly contradicted the Book of Genesis. It was this new account of human origins that caused doubts about the Bible to arise in the popular mind. But in intellectual circles Darwinism was only one aspect of a much more deep-seated change beginning to take place in the collective European mind.

Starting at the Renaissance, with the recovery of the knowledge of ancient Greek and Roman culture and fostered by the Protestant Reformation, there slowly began to develop in the European mind an awareness of history and of historical change. It led, in the eighteenth and nineteenth centuries, to historical research and to the establishment of Professorial Chairs in History at the Universities. The new discipline of history was at first referred to as Modern History, to distinguish it from the history of Greece and Rome, even though it covered everything since that time. The growing sense of history prompted biblical scholars, in turn, to study the bible with the tools of literary and historical criticism. They soon came up with some alarming results such as the inescapable conclusion that Moses did not write 'The Books of Moses', and the clear evidence that the Gospels are not eye-witness accounts of the words and deeds of Jesus.

This sense of history is much more widespread today as a result of the rise of general education in the last two centuries. It has become so much a part of modern thinking that is hard to put ourselves back into the mind-set which prevailed almost universally before the eighteenth century. The knowledge that most people then had about the world in which they lived was confined to their own experience of the present and what they picked up from the Christian based culture in which they lived. They were not nearly so aware of cultural change as we are today. It was natural for them to assume that most of the aspects of life they regarded as important had changed little from the time of creation. There was much in the world that seemed to them to be as changeless as the mountains.

It is true that biblical tradition referred to a few watershed events such as the Great Flood; in particular, the birth of Jesus Christ was thought to have cut history in two. But apart from such world-shattering events, people saw themselves living in a changeless present, marked only by the changing cycle of the seasons, and from this perspective they awaited only the ultimate end of the world.

All this provided people with a certain sense of worldly security. God was in his heaven watching over the world he had made. Catholics could turn to the Pope for authoritative teaching. Protestants could turn to the Bible for the same. In this context, and because of these authorities, it seemed self-evident that the definitions of both God and Christianity were perfectly clear and beyond all doubt.

The new sense of history changed all that. It has been gradually forcing us to step out of a world viewed exclusively through spectacles shaped by the Christian tradition and to move into a larger world, from which we can view the Christian tradition itself from quite a different standpoint. The change has been referred to as 'humankind's coming of age'. It is analogous to the change we experience when on reaching adulthood we move out of our family setting, establish our personal identity in the world, and look back on our parents and our upbringing with new eyes.

Just as we thereupon see our parents and home background more dispassionately, so in the modern world we are now able to view the whole history of humankind from a more objective standpoint. We find that Christianity is one great cultural tradition among others and that the Bible is one set of Holy Scriptures among others. The physical world in which we live is itself neither

Christian nor Buddhist nor Muslim but secular. Here the term 'secular' denotes the tangible, temporal world in which we all live irrespective of our religious beliefs. This is the reality which we all share and which is open to scientific exploration; this world is religiously neutral. As in the past, only our particular interpretations of it make it appear otherwise.

In the light of this new and modern sense of history we are now in a position to understand how the Bible gradually came to be seen as the depository of divine revelation. This view evolved slowly from generation to generation without people being aware of what was happening. One of the first steps was the acceptance of the notion that the oracular utterances of the Israelite prophets were directly communicated to them by God. The oracles were introduced with the words 'Thus spoke the LORD', and in them God spoke in the first person. This direct connection of God with the prophetic oracles was then transferred to the Jewish tradition of the Exodus, associated with Moses. Moses was declared to be a prophet and from about the fifth century B.C.E. onwards the five books of the Torah were assumed to have originated with him. Since the Torah declared, 'There has not arisen a prophet since in Israel like Moses, whom the LORD knew face to face',[9] it was natural to conclude from this that all the material in the book of Genesis had been revealed to Moses by God.

The first Christians inherited from the Jews all their holy scriptures — the Law, the Prophets and the Writings — along with their conviction that 'all scripture is inspired by God and profitable for teaching, for reproof, for correction and for training in righteousness'.[10] For the first two centuries the whole of the Christian Bible consisted of the Jewish Scriptures, including several later books that the Jews eventually abandoned. (They became known as the Apocrypha, after they had been removed from the Bible by the Protestant Reformers). But, in order to establish their own identity as separate from Judaism, Christians found it desirable to add to Holy Scripture their own distinctive writings. These they referred to as the New Testament, relegating the Jewish Bible to the status of the Old Testament. Only those books were chosen for the New Testament, which were at the time believed to have some association with an Apostle.

By the fourth century the Bible had assumed its traditional form (known as the Canon), though some doubt lingered over the Book of Revelation until the sixth century. Thus it was a series of human decisions at various points, which determined what was to be regarded as Holy Scripture. Yet the more Christians became convinced of the divine origin of the Bible the less reason did they have to subject it to criticism. In many ways the Bible continued to demonstrate an inherent validity in the context of contemporary culture. Indeed, the fact that the opening chapters of Genesis could be taken to be historically true for more than two thousand years bears witness to the convincing quality of the story of origins expressed there.

At the same time as the Bible was falling from its pedestal, people began to question the very concept of divine revelation as a channel of reliable information. From time immemorial people have received what knowledge they had from the ongoing cultural tradition into which they were born. To a large extent that is still true. Christian culture had slowly evolved on the basis of Christian teaching. The authoritative conveyer of this tradition was the church, speaking though its clergy and theologians. The theologians contended there were two sources of reliable knowledge — human reasoning and divine revelation. They believed, for example, that it was possible to prove the existence of God by human reasoning. But, for knowledge of what this God is like and what he wills, we humans were said to be dependent on divine revelation. At the core of the Christian tradition, therefore, was a body of revealed knowledge, mostly drawn from the Bible. The Protestant Reformers believed they were on firm ground when they used the Bible, coupled with human reason, to subject the Church to criticism. Two centuries later, the leading thinkers of the Enlightenment (partly because of the new confidence in human reason which resulted from the rediscovery of Greek rationalism at the Renaissance) appealed to human reason to subject the Bible itself to criticism. Eventually, neither the Bible nor the idea of divine revelation could withstand this critique.

Out of this critical process there slowly evolved a new way of establishing a reliable body of knowledge; we refer to it as empirical science. It is too little appreciated that this arose out of the

Christian culture of Western Europe; it was initiated by Christian thinkers and, initially, for Christian purposes. Roger Bacon (1214–1292), who has been named the morning star of modern science wrote that 'the surest method of extirpating all heresies, and of destroying the Kingdom of the anti-Christ, and of establishing true religion in the hearts of men, is by perfecting a true system of natural philosophy'. Later came Francis Bacon (1561–1626); he began to lay the philosophical foundations of empirical science in his books *The Advancement of Learning* and *Novum Organum*. These were later to be followed by the famous *Essay concerning Human Understanding* by the philosopher John Locke (1632–1704). In the meantime there arose a great succession of scientists — Copernicus, Galileo, Kepler and Newton — who were radically changing our mental picture of the universe in which we live. Later yet came such people as Boyle, Maxwell, Darwin, Einstein, and Bohr. Through them our former understanding of the natural world has changed out of all recognition.

At first there was a danger that the rapid erosion of trust in divine revelation as the source of reliable knowledge would result in the setting up of science as the new medium of infallible knowledge. For a while 'Science teaches . . .' seemed to be replacing 'The Pope decrees . . .' or 'The Bible says. . . .' This transition would simply have replaced one idol with another. But, as we came to the end of the twentieth century, more modest claims for the authority of science began to prevail. While the scientific enterprise can certainly lead us to a more reliable body of knowledge of the physical world than did tradition and supposedly divine revelation, it by no means provides us with knowledge which is absolute and final. All scientific knowledge is open to continual review.

The scientific enterprise is a human enterprise. It uses concepts, languages (such as mathematics), and research tools which are of human construction. It is subject to error and to the limitations of the human mind, just as is everything else in human culture. In humankind's coming age we have begun to move beyond the limited boundaries of Christian culture into a broader human culture. (This process is currently occurring with all cultures as a result of globalization). But, as beings who are the products of human culture, there is no way in which we can ever move out of human culture of some kind.

The modern recognition that we humans live within human culture, that we both create human culture and are shaped by it, means that everything in it goes back to something human. (Our common numbering system uses ten as its base simply because we have ten fingers — i.e. digits). Scientific knowledge, the arts, religions, and ethical systems are all of human origin.

Religious claims and theological statements, however valuable and inspiring, can never be more than human attempts to say something of ultimate importance. Therefore they should never be identified with the ultimate truth, but must always remain open to questioning and review. Theology (or God-talk) is highly symbolic. It bears a greater resemblance to poetry than to definitive or descriptive statements. Just as there is good poetry and bad poetry, so there is good theology and bad theology. What may be judged good theology in one age, however, may seem very bad theology in another, for what we humans judge to be of ultimate importance may vary from one age to another.

Moreover theology can be highly deceptive. It can give the appearance of being very profound; yet, on closer examination, it may turn out to be gobbledygook, saying nothing very sensible or meaningful at all. It may even deceive the theologian who wrote it. It is wise to take some theology with a grain of salt. The learned and abstract language engaged in by some academic theologians can have the effect of clouding the issues rather than of clarifying them. One sometimes suspects, for example, that some of those who write this way have beguiled themselves with their own apparent brilliance. Profound yet simple issues can all too easily be fudged by abstract language and made to look more complex than they really are. We should be on our guard. When we find the Emperor has no clothes on we should have the honesty to say so.

That is exactly what some of the ancient Israelite prophets did. One of them poked fun at the religious sacrifices which their fellow Israelites were taking so seriously. The reason why the prophets ridiculed the religious images which some of their contemporaries were worshipping stems from their conviction that a graven image should be recognized for what it is — a humanly made object. Such objects may continue to be valued as symbols but whenever people venerate them or worship them for their own sake they become idolaters. As Bishop John Robinson once pointed out, in modern times it is not so much **metal** images as **mental** images which lead people into idolatry.

Because of all that has just been said, Christianity is today in a more fluid state than it has been since the time of Christian origins. Nothing from its past is any more to be regarded as final and absolute. Everything is open to review and to change. We are free to explore whether or not the traditional idea of God is any longer essential to Christianity. It is not such an absurd question to ask after all.

That does not mean that we are now about to discover the final truth of the matter. Nothing in this book makes any claim to be the final and infallible truth. Readers are encouraged to examine carefully what is written, weigh it in the light of their own experience and decide for themselves whether it has the ring of truth. If we take our beliefs too seriously, we become idolaters just like those from the past whom we often so readily criticise.

So, while what is written here does have a very important and serious intention, it will be mingled with a bit of tongue-in-cheek comment. It is a very healthy practice, from time to time, to laugh at ourselves and our religious creations. So in this book I am first of all going to fly two kites. (What I have called kites are referred to in academic language as theses, the kind of propositions that are presented and defended by the doctoral candidates. If successfully defended and widely accepted by one's peers, they then become part of the accepted knowledge of the culture.) I use the term 'kite' to prevent you from taking anything I say too seriously.

Both kites are on the same string; by that I mean that these two are closely connected. Here they are. I am going to contend:

1. When examined closely, the living stream of Christianity does not, as has been commonly assumed, depend on traditional (theistic) belief in God.
2. Christianity, even in its origins, was already moving towards the rejection of theism.

To fly these kites I shall first examine Christianity and try to determine the most satisfactory way of understanding what it is. Then I shall investigate the origin of the concept of 'God' and the many different ways in which it has been understood. From there we shall explore how Christian doctrine transformed the idea of God into something entirely new and unique. The evolving global culture we live in is the indirect result of this transformation; it may be called 'Christianity without God'.

Chapter Two

What is Christianity?

ntering step by step into today's secular world, Western humankind has had the experience of having its 'Christian world' turned inside out. Previously the whole of reality was viewed from within the 'Christian world' — that is, the world defined by the Christian perspective. We find ourselves now living in a very much larger space-time universe, and one which is religiously neutral (or secular). From this new standpoint we can begin to look at that 'Christian world' from the outside, and when we do so we see it in quite a different way, for we become aware of the Christian spectacles which have long shaped the Western view of reality.

Mediaeval Christians, by contrast, were completely unaware they were looking at the world though lenses tinted by Christian ideas and values. Their history of the world was a Christian history, drawn from the Bible. Their cosmology or mental picture of the universe was a Christian cosmology, based partly on the Bible. We are aware in a way they were not that it was a 'Christian cosmology'. For them it was simply the real world.

It is not surprising, therefore, that it was a change of cosmology which was the first step in the transition from the 'Christian world' to the modern secular world. By introducing the idea of a solar system in the heavens, Copernicus and Galileo displaced the earth from the centre of the universe. Everyone knows how church authorities felt threatened by that. Other implications of the new cosmology were even more shattering, however, and Christians are still working their way through them. What does it mean, for example to say that Jesus descended into the underworld of the dead and later ascended into heaven? We should not be surprised that it is taking Christians so long to become adjusted to the new cosmology; after all, we still talk about the sun 'rising in the East' and 'setting in the West'.

The new cosmology was only one factor among others in leading Westerners out of the mediaeval 'Christian world' into what we now take to be the real world. The more we realise our forbears were viewing reality through Christian spectacles, the more our attention turns to the 'Christian spectacles' themselves, in order to subject them to close scrutiny.

This is why it is really only from the sixteenth century that people began to talk about an entity they called Christianity. Before that time people in Christendom talked about the church or about faith (by which they meant Christian faith) or about religion (by which they meant devotion), but never about something known as Christianity. The founding document of the Church of England (1562) was not called 'A Manual of Christianity" but 'Articles for the Establishing of Consent touching True Religion'. In them there is an occasional reference to 'Christian men' (*sic*), but none to 'Christianity'.

It is no accident that the first books to be written specifically about 'Christianity' appeared in the eighteenth century, just as the modern world was beginning to emerge. Two of the most famous (some would say infamous) were John Toland's *Christianity not Mysterious* (1696), and William Tindal's *Christianity as Old as the Creation* (1730). These and other leading thinkers of what became known as the Enlightenment (or Age of Reason) still claimed to be Christian. But they were beginning to look more objectively at the Christian culture which had shaped them and to subject to rational examination what I have referred to as the 'Christian spectacles'. These consisted of the concepts, ideas, stories, and doctrines which gave shape to the 'Christian world'. They referred to these as 'Christianity'.

The word Christianity is derived from the medieval Latin *Christianitas*. It was originally a synonym for Christendom, meaning the geographical domain where Christ ruled. It now came to refer to the Christian beliefs and practices which gave the Christian culture of this domain its distinctive character.

Thus the way we use the word 'Christianity' today is comparatively modern and reflects a process which Wilfred Cantwell Smith, an American scholar of international repute, has called the 'reification' of religion.[1] This means that 'religion' in general, and 'Christianity' in particular, are now too often being treated as 'things'.

Up until the sixteenth century 'religion' was synonymous with 'devotion' and referred to the feelings of awe and wonder, which along with the attitudes of trust and love, constitute the religious life. 'Religion' was an abstract term which could not be used in the plural. People began to speak of 'religions' only after the word had been reified and come to mean the beliefs, practices, and institutions in which such devotion manifests itself. In particular it referred to a set of ideas, an ideology, which one could choose to embrace or reject, as the case may be. As 'religion' in general became thus objectified, so particular names were needed to refer to the variety of forms it could take. Religion or devotion was expressed in a variety of specific 'religions' and these needed to be named. That is why such terms as Christianity and Judaism began to come into common use, followed in the nineteenth century by Buddhism, Hinduism, Confucianism, etc.

This growing practice of treating Christianity as an objective entity then gave rise to the problem of defining it. What is this thing called Christianity? What does one have to believe and do to be a Christian? Does it mean belonging to an institution, such as the church? Does it mean holding a clearly defined set of beliefs? If so, what are these beliefs?

These questions were proving very difficult to answer. Already from the Protestant Reformation onwards, it was very clear that Christians could be equally sincere and devout and yet hold quite different beliefs and belong to different churches. Thinkers such as the above mentioned Toland and Tindal were the most radical. They contended that Christianity did not depend on supernatural miracles but consisted of some simple basic truths which could be arrived at by the use of reason. They reduced such beliefs to 'the existence of God' and 'the obligation to live a moral life, for which there would be reward or punishment in the after-life'.

But while most people believed that Christianity also includes a belief system, as expressed in the historic Creeds and Confessions, beyond that they could not agree. Catholics insisted that Christianity consists of giving obedience to the Pope and living a sacramental life within Mother Church. Protestant evangelicals believed Christianity consists of accepting Jesus Christ as one's personal Lord and Saviour. By the end of the nineteenth century, on the other hand, very liberal Christians were already reducing Christianity to a set of moral values by which to live.

In short, Christians were becoming hopelessly divided on just what this thing is that we call Christianity, and the problem was intensified by the emergence of the modern world. Some beliefs held by Christians at earlier times were now coming under severe criticism. It was clear that some things had to change, but if so, what? While the very conservative argued that nothing at all could possibly be changed, the main body of Christians argued that though some change was necessary, there were certain unchangeable truths which must be preserved at all costs. They searched for the essence or *sine qua non* of Christianity.

The attempt to find the essence of Christianity may be said to have reached an interesting high point with the publication in 1900 of a widely read little book by the famous church historian Adolf Harnack. The German title meant 'The Essence of Christianity' but its English translation was *What is Christianity?* After stripping away the excrescences which had come to hide the essence of Christianity, he concluded, 'The Christian religion is something simple and sublime; it means one thing and one thing only; eternal life in the midst of time, by the strength and under the eyes of God'.[2] Elsewhere he described this in terms of loving God and loving one's neighbour.

Although this book received enthusiastic acclaim and was widely influential, many thought it to be inadequate and reductionist. One of his chief critics was the Catholic Modernist Alfred Loisy (1858–1940). In his book *L'Évangile et L'Église* (The Church and the Gospel), 1902, Loisy set out to defend Catholicism against the Protestant Liberalism of Harnack. Taking a quite different approach, he argued that though Christ neither founded the Church nor instituted the Sacraments, it was perfectly legitimate for Christian faith to have developed in the more complex way it had. The essence of Christianity, said Loisy, is not to be found in any objective doctrine or practice but in the ongoing experience of faith in the hearts and lives of Christians. (Loisy found himself immediately condemned by the Catholic Hierarchy and was soon after excommunicated. He went on to become a brilliant scholar in the history of religion.) Loisy had put his finger upon a new and important model for understanding not only Christianity but every religious tradition.

Loisy was arguing that in trying to isolate the essence of Christianity, Harnack had said both too little and too much. Harnack had said too little in that at any one time in history Christianity was much more than the simple formula he had arrived at. But Harnack had also claimed too much in contending there is some absolute and unchangeable objective content to be found in the long and complex story of Christianity. For Loisy, Christianity was not a permanent, static entity but a developing process.

Wilfred Cantwell Smith may not have been aware of Loisy's insights (for he does not mention him) and yet he expounded very similar emphases in his seminal little book, *The Meaning and End of Religion, A New Approach to the Religious Traditions of Mankind*. Smith even suggested we should stop asking the question 'What is Christianity?' for it too often carries the assumption that somewhere, hidden amid unessentials, there is a simple and precise thing (such as some fundamental doctrine) which can be recovered in its pristine purity. 'What is Christianity?' thus comes to be seen as a loaded question, not unlike the hoary chestnut 'Have you stopped beating your wife?'

Smith suggested that instead of using the term 'Christianity', we should refer on the one hand to faith (an inner experience universal to the human condition) and on the other hand to the form which faith has taken during the course of history; this he termed the 'cumulative tradition'. He thus drew a sharp distinction between faith and the products of faith. By the 'Christian cumulative tradition' he meant the objective data (such as Holy Scriptures, creeds, doctrines, rituals, and social institutions) which may be explored by the historian of religion. It encompasses everything thought and done by all who thought themselves to be Christian; and to avoid being judgmental, the historian must include what the main body of Christians have judged to be deviances or heresies.

Smith argued that the reification of Christianity (as exemplified in the identification of faith with the Christian cumulative tradition) has been an unfortunate and misleading modern trend. It had led to the widespread perception that Christian faith consists of holding a certain number of unchangeable doctrines and beliefs. This makes a mockery of Christian faith and reduces it to the schoolboy's caricature — 'Faith is believing things you know ain't true'.

It was this modern error of equating faith with holding certain beliefs that Lewis Carroll poked fun at in 1865 when he wrote *Alice in Wonderland*. There he portrayed Alice as saying, 'I can't possibly believe that!' The Queen replied, 'Perhaps you haven't had enough practice. Why, I have believed as many as six impossible things before breakfast'.

This tendency arose in the nineteenth and twentieth centuries because during that time our general beliefs were changing so rapidly. It is less than two hundred years since nearly everyone in the Western world believed the earth was only six thousand years old and that we were all descended from two common ancestors, Adam and Eve. Those are only two of a whole host of beliefs held by all Christians before 1800 but rejected by all well-informed people today. Because these and other now outmoded beliefs had long been woven into what Christians believed in former generations, far too many people supposed that to be a Christian one had to continue believing what all earlier Christians had believed.

Part of the confusion has arisen from the fact that our word 'belief' has somewhat changed in meaning and usage since earlier times. When people today say 'I believe in God', they generally mean that in their opinion a spiritual being called God exists. That is not what it meant four centuries ago; indeed, the existence of such a God was commonly regarded as a self-evident fact. 'To believe in God', in those days, meant 'to put one's trust in God'. A remnant of this meaning is still present in the phrase 'I believe you'. This change of meaning can be clearly illustrated: we often hear conservative Christians today say they 'believe in the Devil'.

No sixteenth-century Christian would have dreamed of saying such a dreadful thing. Of course it was their opinion that the Devil existed. But in those days to say 'I believe in the Devil' meant 'I give my allegiance to the devil'.

The beliefs we hold at any given time depend largely on the culture which has shaped us. If we had lived in the middle ages, we would almost certainly have believed that the earth was flat and probably that the stars were the lights of heaven. We would not only have believed in the existence of God but also in the existence of angels, spirits and the Devil, to say nothing of hobgoblins and fairies. These were all part of the body of the many beliefs which made up the mediaeval view of reality. Our beliefs at any one time reflect the century in which we live and the culture in which we have been nurtured.

Furthermore, our beliefs are not embraced by choice. That is why people often declare, 'I cannot possibly believe that!' Our beliefs take shape in us as a result both of our experience and of the impact of our cultural tradition upon us. We should be left free from external constraints to formulate our beliefs in the way that best preserves our honesty and integrity. We rightly resist having other people's beliefs imposed upon us, for that would lead us into a state of intellectual slavery, turned, as it were, into a ventriloquist's dummy.

Even though it may be closely connected with one's beliefs, faith is something altogether different from belief. Abraham, Jeremiah, Jesus, Paul, Augustine, and Luther were all people of faith; but their beliefs varied tremendously. The closest synonym of faith, therefore, is not belief but trust. Faith is a total response of trust towards the world in general, towards people, and towards the future. That is why faith has a strong affinity with hope. This is reflected in the letter to the Hebrews, 'Faith is the assurance of things hoped for', and in the famous hymn where Paul placed it in his trinity of eternal values — faith, hope, and love.

Faith is also closely allied with integrity. Integrity means wholeness. It abhors intellectual contradictions and moral inconsistency. To embrace openly beliefs which you may secretly doubt is thus the very opposite of faith, for it means that you are at cross-purposes with yourself. This is well illustrated by a well-known verse from the prophet Habakkuk. It is commonly translated as

'The just shall live by his faith'[3]. A better translation would be, 'The righteous man shall live by reason of his integrity'. The word translated as 'faith' or 'integrity' has to do with steadfastness, fidelity, reliability. It comes from the same Hebrew root as the word 'Amen'. And it is this idea which lies behind the references to faith in the New Testament, as when Jesus said to the woman who clutched at his garment in the hope of being made well, 'It is your faith that has made you whole'.[4]

As Smith has well said,

> Faith is a quality of human living. At its best it has taken the form of serenity and courage and service; a quiet confidence and joy that enable one to feel at home in the universe, and to find meaning in the world and in one's life, a meaning that is profound and ultimate, and is stable no matter what may happen to oneself at the level of immediate event.[5]

Once we distinguish between faith and the holding of certain beliefs Christian faith can be seen in quite a new light. The very act of discarding outworn beliefs, far from demonstrating a lack of faith, may in fact be just the opposite. It may open the door for genuine faith to operate again. Indeed, the modern atheist who rejects the notion of God in the interests of truth may be manifesting more faith than the traditional theist. The assertion that one needs to believe a particular creed or set of doctrines in order to have faith is an invitation not to faith but to credulity. There is a world of difference between child-like faith and childish credulity.

In a remarkable little book, *The Faith to Doubt*, M. Holmes Hartshorne wrote,

> People today are not in need of assurances about the truth of doubtful beliefs. They need the courage to doubt. They need the faith by which to reject their idols. The churches cannot preach to this age if they stand outside of it, living in the illusory security of yesterday's beliefs. These lie about us broken, and we cannot by taking thought raise them from the dead.[6]

Doubt is not the enemy of faith but its ally, as the enemy of false beliefs. All beliefs should be continually subjected to doubt and critical examination and, when found to be false or inadequate, they should be discarded. The faith so essential to the Christian is of quite a different order and has long been symbolized in the figure of Abraham. Whatever his beliefs, they were certainly very different from ours. He knew nothing about Moses, yet he is honoured by the Jews as their spiritual father. He knew nothing about the Qur'an but is honoured by Islam as the first Muslim. He knew nothing about Jesus Christ, yet the first Christians honoured him as the very model of a man of faith.[7]

The influence of Smith in leading us to a better understanding of religion is well illustrated by the difference between the titles of two books which have substantially the same content. In 1949 John B. Noss wrote a descriptive history of the chief religious traditions of the world. It has been widely used as a university textbook and has gone through many editions. He called it *Man's Religions*. In 1969, not long after the publication of Smith's book, John A. Hutchison wrote a very similar book but called it *Paths of Faith*. To understand any religious tradition it is fruitful to see it as a path trodden by a person or community of faith.

I wish to suggest another simile, one which attempts to acknowledge both the component of personal faith and the close relationship between religion and culture. Let us liken Christianity to a river and see it as a stream of living culture flowing through the plains of time. As it flows onward it gathers new material from the banks it passes between. Sometimes objects may crystallize within it. Sometimes it leaves these objects on the bank, together with various sediments it has been carrying along. There is a tendency for people to regard the more visible objects in the Christian cultural stream (such as beliefs, creeds, institutions, and even the Bible) as being of the essence of the stream. Yet none of them has the permanence of the stream which carries them along.

Further, just like the rivers coming down from great mountain ranges and flowing through plains, a cultural stream may not only be joined by other streams but also divide into branches before later rejoining. As it gets nearer to the sea, it may even form a delta of many streams, each with its own mouth.

The Christian cultural stream has its source in the traditions of ancient Israel whose cultural stream eventually gave rise to three broad streams — rabbinical Judaism, Christianity, and Islam. Each claimed the patriarchs and Israelite prophets as part of their own tradition. As a Jewish scholar once shrewdly observed, 'Islam is really Judaism *transplanted* among the Arabs and Christianity is really Judaism *transformed* for the Gentiles'.[8]

Even the pre-Christian Jewish stream was already much more multi-cultural in origin than its Holy Scriptures tend to imply. From the sixth century B.C.E. onwards, it was penetrated by tributaries from Persian Zoroastrianism and Hellenism. Much of these two lives on *incognito* in the Jewish, Christian, and Islamic streams.

To the influence of the Zoroastrian tradition, for example, we owe such ideas as the Last Judgment (preceded by a general resurrection), an after-life with rewards and punishments, the concept of a personal Devil, the writing of our life story in a heavenly book of life, and the naming of angels with specific functions.

The stimulating influence of Jesus of Nazareth had the effect of adding such a fresh burst of vitality to the Jewish cultural stream that it caused part of it to break out of its banks and form a new stream, which we now commonly refer to as the Christian tradition. It took with it the Jewish Scriptures, the monotheistic God, and the institution of the synagogue. Even the Eucharist probably owes something to an ancient synagogue rite of sharing food and wine.

At the beginning of the Christian era, the Jewish tradition had no intention of giving birth to the Christian stream. The new Jewish sect known as 'the Christians'[9] was regarded as an heretical movement even though its key figure, Jesus of Nazareth, and his chief interpreter, Paul, were both Jewish to the core. And a number of early Christians did not see their movement as the abandonment of the Jewish tradition but as its fulfilment. Matthew, for example, represented Jesus as saying, 'I have come not to abolish the law and the prophets but to fulfil them'.[10]

But as the new and vigorous Christian movement overflowed the banks of the Jewish stream and began to spread into the Gentile world around the Mediterranean, it picked up new and significant ingredients from the Greek and Roman cultural traditions. Philosophical terms (such as the *Logos*), analytical reasoning, a different understanding of the human condition, new notions of God, and even the intellectual discipline known as theology — all these came from the Greeks. Legal and organizational strengths came from the Romans. Indeed, the reason why the church eventually split into Eastern Orthodox and Western Catholic branches owes much to the fact that Greek culture permeated the former and Roman culture dominated the latter. The Western Church fell heir to the legacy of the fallen Roman Empire, with the Pope assuming the mantle of the Emperor by taking the latter's title of Pontifex Maximus.

In addition, the quickly developing Christian stream encountered many competitors such as the mystery religions, Gnosticism, and Manichaeism; and these also left visible traces as they mingled with the Christian stream. For example, Augustine, the chief theologian of the early Western church, was a Manichaeist for nine years before returning to the Christian faith of his mother; he could not wholly disengage himself from his Manichaeist experience, and some of it, such as his negative understanding of sexuality, he took with him.

Of all the streams then flowing into the declining Graeco-Roman Mediterranean culture, the Christian one eventually proved to be the most enduring, and as it spread and consolidated, it created Christendom. We call it Christian culture because dominant within this stream were the ideas, values, myths, and goals, which had come to be associated with the name Jesus Christ. Although many of these concepts and beliefs had originated both before and after the man Jesus, they became part of the complex stream much later to be called Christianity and were stamped with the Christian label.

As we look back over two thousand years of Christian history (to say nothing of four thousand years of the Judeo-Christian stream as a whole), we can readily discern distinctive phases, each with its own particular emphases and characteristics. What was regarded to be of essential importance in one phase could almost disappear from view in another phase.

The first Christians, being Jewish, believed it to be vitally important to preserve Jewish practices, as Jesus himself had done. Largely as a result of Paul's influence and the destruction of Jerusalem in 70 C.E., it was the Gentile wing of the church which won the day; and the Jewish Christians (who denied the Virgin Birth, used only St. Matthew's Gospel, and rejected Paul's teaching) were eventually judged to be heretics by the Gentile church, and their community faded out by the end of the fifth century.

The Gentile Christian stream, having become disjoined from the Jewish stream, had to find a way of re-structuring its thinking to be convincing to the Greek mentality. The problem that became uppermost in the Christian stream was how to reconcile the humanity of Jesus with his divinity. One writer of the day complained that one could not even visit the baker to buy a loaf of bread without being caught up in some theological debate. One such dispute turned on whether the proper word to describe the relationship of Jesus Christ to God the Father was *homoousios* or *homoiousios* — of one substance or of similar substance. (From this debate may come the common saying 'It does not make an iota of difference!') But as soon as these problems were settled by ecumenical councils (though only by a majority vote, which could have the effect of excommunicating those who disagreed) the issues began to recede into the background. Nevertheless they are part of the baggage which the church has carried down to the present day.

During the Middle Ages any interest in the theological debates of the first five centuries was confined, when it existed at all, to a very few intellectuals. The Christian stream spread and flourished very much at the level of folk religion, with one or another of the Saints along with the Virgin Mary commonly the focal point of devotion; God was regarded as being altogether too distant to be of help to the ordinary person. Another dominant interest was the concept of Purgatory. Although this did not figure at all in the early centuries, by the late Middle Ages it had become one of the most important doctrines, since that was where most Christians expected to go when they died.

The Protestant Reformation was felt by Catholics to be an open assault on the Christian faith, partly because it abolished the doctrine of Purgatory with one fell swoop. When accused by Catholics of being heretics and apostates, the Protestants responded by referring to the Catholic Church as the synagogue of Satan, and the Pope as the 'antichrist, that man of sin and son of perdition'.[11] For nearly four hundred years neither Catholics nor Protestants acknowledged one another as Christian. This meant that the Western Christian stream, while contained within the one broad cultural riverbed, had divided into two (and eventually more) streams, separated by powerful currents of distrust, and largely blind to the large amount of cultural heritage they still possessed in common.

At each new phase in the developing stream of Christian culture, some have strongly resisted change, believing it entailed the loss of something essential to its nature. Time enables us to put those things into perspective. Back in the second century, as the long tradition of anti-Semitic hostility was beginning, who would have thought that, following the Nazi Holocaust, Jewish-Christian relations would have reached today's level of mutual understanding and respect?

During the religious wars of the sixteenth and seventeenth centuries, who would have thought that Protestant and Catholic streams would ever reach the rapprochement that has occurred since the Vatican II Council? The remaining differences, while still real, have greatly diminished in importance because of the acknowledgment of what they have in common.

We should keep this in mind as we now look at the most recent change taking place in the Christian cultural stream. During the last four hundred years, western Christendom has entered a new phase as a result of the new thinking of the Enlightenment, the rise of empirical science, and the development of new technology. Out of the Christian West is emerging the modern secular and global world.[12]

The modern secular world, with all its faults and problems, represents a new but legitimate stage in the Judeo-Christian cultural stream, just as Gentile Christianity, mediaeval Christendom, and Protestantism were new phases in their eras. Certainly the coming of the global secular world entails the end of much of the ossified structure known as Christian orthodoxy, but that should not be regarded as the *sine qua non* of the Christian stream.

The people who pioneered the modern secular world were not bishops and popes (just as Paul, the pioneer of Gentile Christianity, was not one of the twelve Apostles!). Here are a few of them — Francis of Assisi, Roger Bacon, William of Ockham, Erasmus, John Wyclif, Copernicus, Galileo, Francis Bacon, Isaac Newton, David Strauss, Ludwig Feuerbach, Charles Darwin. They were on the Christian margins, rather than at the centre of Christian officialdom. But they never regarded themselves as in any sense the enemies of Christianity. On the contrary, they were not only theologically literate but regarded themselves firmly rooted within the Christian tradition. They were simply pursuing truth wherever it led them in the quest to discover the laws of nature. They did not intentionally or even knowingly lead the way to modern secularization. Yet, step by step, they were turning the Christian stream in that direction.

Take, for example, Francis of Assisi (1181–1226), hailed today as patron saint by secular conservationists. He was the first to reverse the Christian attitude toward the world of nature from one of negative devaluation to one of positive appreciation. Furthermore, he founded the Franciscan Order, out of which came such pioneers of empirical science as Roger Bacon (1214–1292) and the founders of modern philosophy such as William of Ockham. Ockham's nominalist philosophy, known as the *via moderna,* not only influenced Luther but also laid the foundations of the materialist and non-realist philosophies of the nineteenth and twentieth centuries.

As Francis and his successors revalued the physical earth upwards, so the humanists of the Renaissance, such as Erasmus (1466–1536), laid the basis for a more positive evaluation of the human condition. Although the revaluing of the earth and humanity appeared at first to be a clear rejection of such long-standing Christian beliefs as the fallen state of nature and the sinfulness of humankind, we find to our surprise that, in some respects, it actually brings us even closer to the beliefs of primitive Christians than medieval Christians were.

The modern secular world is therefore not the anti-Christian enemy it is often made out to be by some church officials; it is the logical continuation of the Judeo-Christian cultural stream. In its new course, that stream has not given rise to a new organization, as it did in the past. That is partly why we have been unable to get a clear understanding of what has been happening. As people have increasingly questioned and abandoned specific Christian beliefs and practices of the past they have been slowly disengaging themselves from the organization of the church. They have become the 'unchurched' or what Bishop Spong has called 'the church's alumni association'. Although they have not established a new organization to replace the church they have, often unknowingly, been building a new kind of society — a global secular society.

Not only in the West, but in other cultures also, people have been freeing themselves from their past cultural conventions and religious beliefs, proclaiming their common humanity (see, for example, The Declaration of Human Rights), acknowledging their responsibilities to one another and to the earth, and putting into place the legal and commercial organizations desirable for the new global society. This emerging secular world is not Christian in the way the mediaeval 'Christian world' was. But neither is it anti-Christian. It is rightly called 'post-Christian', a term which indicates both its indebtedness to its Christian roots and its new character. It is post-Christian in much the same way as the newly emerging Christian stream of the ancient world was post-Jewish.

In this global secular world, the kind of faith described above by Wilfred Cantwell Smith is not only possible but necessary. The once separate paths of faith are increasingly meeting; the cultural streams are flowing together. Whether the resulting stream may still be called Christian is largely a semantic issue. It is certainly in continuity with the Christian stream of the past. The chief difference is that the surrounding scenery has changed. The cosmic superstructure of the 'Christian world' is disappearing from view. It was created by ancient Christian imagination in the early centuries out of the raw material of the three-decker cosmology which prevailed in the ancient world. The idea of a post-mortem existence in Purgatory, hell, or heaven is no longer tenable or meaningful.

Ever since the Enlightenment the dualistic dichotomy of eternal/temporal, spiritual/material, heavenly/earthly, divine/human has been coming under close scrutiny. Much of it has already disappeared or been re-interpreted. Basic to this dichotomy has been the concept of God. What is the future of God? To that we now turn.

Chapter Three

Who made God?

any people in the Western world first heard the word God when it was used to answer some of their earliest questions: Who made the flowers? Who made the birds? Who made the stars? And above all, Who made the world? They were told that it is God who made the world. The answer was faithful to the Bible, which begins — 'In the beginning God created the heaven and the earth'. It was faithful to the Creeds, which affirm God as the 'Maker of heaven and earth'.

Some inquiring childish minds, not wholly satisfied with that answer, go on to ask, 'But who made God?' That question has sometimes had parents stumped for an answer. Some have replied that God made himself. Others (perhaps more correctly) have said that God was never made. But even these answers may not satisfy the most sophisticated mind since they lead to further quite legitimate questions. If God was neither made nor made himself, why bring in God at all in order to answer the question? Why not simply say either that the world made itself, or that it was never made? Scientists have long since dropped the practice of appealing to God as the answer to their questions. Moreover they have led us to understand how the universe operates according to its own internal laws — laws that even explain the very slow evolution of life on this tiny planet. Thus, we can now simply say that we live in a self-evolving universe that appears to have no need of a divine creator to explain either its existence or its continuing operation. To say this may not necessarily be true, but it is not nearly so nonsensical as it once appeared to be.

In any case, as we leave behind the world as it appeared through 'Christian spectacles', begin to appreciate the vastness of this space-time universe, and gain some knowledge of the evolution of human language and culture, we are in a better position to discuss the question 'Who made God?' It is now possible even to sketch the history of God — that is, the history of the human notion of God from its origin until now.

Few have done this better than Karen Armstrong, who in 1993 wrote *A History of God*. She herself had made a dramatic personal journey into the modern secular world out of the intensely pious Catholic background of her youth (including five years as a nun), and this existential odyssey (which she had previously made public) recapitulated in well less than a single lifetime what has been occurring in Western culture over the last three hundred years. Even only two centuries ago the title of her book would have been thought sacrilegious. Perhaps it was fear of that which prompted the publishers at first to turn it down; in any case they said it would not sell. In fact, it became a best-seller.

A History of God confines itself to the story of monotheism — the belief that there is one and only one God — which has long been regarded as the foundation of the three intertwined paths of faith we know as Judaism, Christianity, and Islam. So her book is sub-titled 'From Abraham to the Present: the 4000-year quest for God'. In this book, however, we shall attempt to go back even further, to the time when the very concept of a god began to form in the human mind.

Until relatively recently we were not even prompted to raise the issue, let alone be in a position to discuss it. In the 'Christian world' the reality of God seemed to be self-evident. Even as late as 1535 John Calvin could write, 'That there exists in the human mind, and indeed by natural instinct, some sense of Deity, we hold to be beyond dispute, since God Himself . . . has imbued all men with some idea of his Godhead . . . There is no nation so barbarous, no race so brutish, as not to be imbued with the conviction that there is a God.'[1] In the 'Christian world' in which Calvin lived, there was every reason to believe that human knowledge of God went back to the time of Adam and Eve. Had not God revealed himself to our first parents and spoken to them face to face?

In the greatly expanded and multi-cultural world in which we live, Calvin's claim is seriously flawed. 'The conviction that there is a God' has never been universal to humankind. Behind the concept of God (as now found in Western culture) there lies a long and complex history. It is possible to sketch this in outline even though our knowledge of the origins of human culture is very hazy and some of our reconstruction has to be in the nature of surmise.

Reliable knowledge of what the earliest humans actually thought and said goes back only as far as the invention of writing, some five or six thousand years ago. By that time human language of some kind had probably been in existence for a hundred thousand years and perhaps much longer.[2] As already noted in chapter 1, because language evolved in tandem with the human condition, it is not surprising that our earliest known myths assumed language to have been there from the beginning.

We now know that languages evolve, that new words are coined, that meanings change, and that some words fall out of use altogether. We also know that because of the experience common to all humans irrespective of their race, many of the same basic concepts are found in most languages even though they are expressed by different words. At what point, then, and for what reason did the concept of 'god' first come to be formed by the human mind?

It is reasonable to conclude that though human language may have begun with emotional cries of various kinds (just as animal languages do), the first words created by humans to convey some cognitive meaning were those which named visible objects. We call these concrete nouns. We have only to observe infants just beginning to speak; the first words they use denote the persons and objects most important to them. Sometimes they invent their own naming words, even before learning the already existing words of their mother tongue. Since gods are not visible objects, the concept of a 'god' can hardly, therefore, have belonged to the earliest stage of language. Even today the use of the term 'God' springs from our culture and not from our observation of something we wish to name.

So how did the idea of a 'god' arise? Let us try to recapture the mindset of our earliest human ancestors in so far as we can get some idea of this from tribal cultures and from the earliest known artifacts and writings. The ancients did not see the inanimate world of nature in the same way as we do. They observed the same phenomena of nature — mountains, running water, growing vegetation, wind, storms, the rising sun, the changing seasons — but they perceived it very differently, both emotionally and intellectually. They experienced their external environment as a unified world, wholly permeated by invisible power. We are left to surmise about the way they created concepts and words to interpret what they saw and felt. By the time extant written records tell us anything, there had been a long evolution of the story-telling by which they interpreted what they encountered. These stories we call their mythology; innumerable spirits and gods had already long been a part of it.

The oldest myths in the Bible take us only a short way back towards that very distant past. Yet even they can help us. There was one particular phenomenon of nature in which the mysterious power almost became tangible though not actually visible, and that was in wind and/or breath. At that stage there was no understanding of gas as a physical state of matter, comparable to that of liquids and solids. The word invented by the ancients meant both 'breath' and 'wind'; but it also denoted the mysterious power which permeated and surrounded all visible objects. Thus it was that the Hebrew *ruach*, the Greek *pneuma* and the Latin *spiritus* each had multiple meanings in their respective cultures. This ambiguity was employed by biblical authors; in John 3, for example, English versions translate the same word *pneuma*, sometimes as 'wind' and sometimes as 'spirit'.

Further, there was thought to be an intrinsic connection between wind/breath/spirit and life. A dead person no longer breathes, for the breath/spirit has departed. 'When God formed Adam (humankind) out of the dust of the ground, he breathed into his nostrils the breath of life and Adam became a living being'.[3] When humans die, 'the dust returns to the earth as it was and the breath/spirit returns to God who gave it'.[4] Wind, breath, spirit and life all pointed to awesome, mysterious power beyond human control. This power held great fascination for the developing human mind; people felt it was to be both feared and wor-shipped (i.e. highly valued).

As Rudolf Otto set out to show in his seminal book *The Idea of the Holy* (1923), all religion probably arose out of the over-whelming experience of this mysterious power. It is reasonable to conclude that the verbal concepts early humans created in relation to it were at first vague, impersonal, and undifferentiated, much like the Japanese *kami* and the Maori *mana*, which have survived to this day.

In modern Maori society mana has become almost equiva-lent to prestige or status, but in earlier times it was a mysterious essence of power. It could be received at birth, transferred from a father to a son, or from a teacher to a pupil, and even transferred to objects such as the kumara (potato) in the first planting of the season, or to a stone or tree which serves as a boundary-marker. Mana, being supernatural power, could be dangerous. Great care had to be taken to protect oneself from it, just as we do wherever there is reason to suspect live electricity or nuclear energy. Like electricity and nuclear energy, mana was an impersonal power even though it could reside in persons. Equally impersonal in the ancient world were the words that expressed sacredness and holiness.

The power exerted by holiness is well illustrated by the pre-cautions required when dealing with particular things, places or people believed to be holy. In the ancient Semitic world the word *qadosh* (later translated as 'holy') was used of those places, objects, and people in whom this mysterious power was thought to oper-ate. One had to take great care in approaching them. When Uzzah instinctively put out his hand to prevent the ark of the covenant from falling, he died on the spot.[5] The garments worn by priests (such as copes and surplices), though later often treated as status symbols and badges of honour, originated as equipment designed to protect the priest when entering holy precincts and handling holy objects.

The holy or sacred power necessitated a response from people quite unlike the unemotional and impersonal way in which we today handle inanimate objects, and much more like the way we respond to other people and sense their presence. In the latter there is a reciprocity, since both parties feel they may change as a result of the encounter. It was that kind of personal reciprocity which the ancients experienced as they encountered what they conceived to be holy and mysterious power. They began to treat this power as if it possessed the same personal and subjective qualities as they themselves did. (We may compare this to the way in which a little child, accidentally knocking against a table and feeling pain, turns round and says, 'You naughty table!') Thus the mysterious forces of the natural world took on personal characteristics. They began to be treated by the ancients as if they operated according to the emotions, whims, and intentions of a personal will similar to their own.

Drawing on our modern understanding of the human psyche, we can say that the ancients projected their subjective experience onto their environment, yet not in such a way as to be aware that they were doing so. They simply encountered their environment with awe because of its mysterious power. Their conception of the world was shaped by what they felt inwardly; they saw the external world as a mirror reflection of their inner world.

As the ancients projected their own feelings and other personal characteristics on to the external world, there came to birth in the primitive human mind a class of invisible and person-like beings. The ancients did not ask **what** caused the storm but **who** caused it. To them it seemed self-evident that all natural events, such as storms, were caused by personal wills, similar to their own. They gave names to these unseen personal beings, such as Agni (fire), Mazda (light), Thor (thunder).

As there seemed to be many of these beings they needed general words to refer to them as a class. Various words or concepts came into use for this purpose, yet it seems quite likely (though we cannot be sure) that the proper names came into use before the generic term which linked them into a class. One such term was 'lords', simply because these were powers which had to be obeyed. The two most widespread terms which have come down to us are 'spirits' (for they were like the powerful but invisible wind) and 'gods'. Thus were the gods conceived, created and named, by the collective human mind. It was all made possible through language and human imagination. At that stage the word 'god', being an abstract generic term, was a common noun.

There were many common elements in the polytheistic cultures which evolved, simply because the external world was basically the same everywhere. The earth was spoken of as Mother, and the Sky as Father (still reflected in the words 'our heavenly Father'). Also projected onto this class of spiritual beings — the gods — were human sexuality and human family relationships.

One of the first to realise what had been happening in the primitive world was the Greek philosopher Xenophanes (sixth century B.C.E.). He condemned the Olympian gods for their immorality, poked fun at their anthropomorphic character, and argued that animals probably made gods in their own image as much as humans had done. At about the same time the Israelite prophets were scornfully dismissing the gods of the nations as having no reality or substance to them.

But Xenophanes and the Israelite prophets bring us to a great threshold of cultural change in the history of human culture. This is now commonly referred to as the Axial Period[6] (800-200 B.C.E.), for it is just as if human culture took a giant turn on its axis. It was to prove a severe testing period for the gods; their fortunes varied from culture to culture. In those areas untouched by the Axial Period, such as Africa, the Americas, and Oceania, the gods survived in human culture until modern times. But in Asia (and Europe) the Axial Period increasingly brought about the end of the gods.

Gautama the Buddha did not even bother to deny the existence of the gods. He simply displaced them from the place of prominence and control to which they had been raised, and, because he regarded them as irrelevant to the human religious quest, they eventually faded from Buddhist consciousness and terminology. By the same token, as Buddhism permeated other cultures, figures very like the ancient gods began to re-appear. But that is another story and simply reflects how the post-Axial traditions have always shown a tendency to revert to pre-Axial forms. The fact remains that the Buddhist tradition, older than Christianity by some 500 years, abandoned the concept of the gods and successfully provided an alternative 'mode of the interpreting and living of life',[7] thus demonstrating that the gods were dispensable to religion.

Whereas the Buddha simply ignored the gods, the Israelite prophets quite openly attacked them. At first they did not deny the reality of the gods which other nations worshipped but were content to restrict their own allegiance to the one god, whom they called YHWH (Yahweh).[8] This god was said to have declared: 'You shall have no other gods besides me'.[9] (The situation in which each nation is reckoned to have its own god is not yet pure monotheism and is sometimes referred to as henotheism.)

Through most of the period of classical Israel, 1000 – 597 B.C.E., the Israelite prophets were fighting the last remnants of polytheism among their people, warning them not 'to go after other gods to their own hurt'.[10] Not until the sixth century B.C.E. did an anonymous prophetic voice proclaim that Yahweh was the only god who had any reality. 'Turn to me and be saved, all the ends of the earth! For I am God, and **there is no other**'.[11] This prophet then proceeded to poke fun at 'the gods' (of other nations), declaring that they had no substance or reality and that, in so far as they are identifiable by their images, they were quite clearly human creations.[12]

When the Israelites denounced the gods of the nations they retained the proper name of their ancestral god YHWH and affirmed him to be the one and only God. We do not know the origin of this proper name. Some think it may be the name of a Semitic storm god. The Bible itself offers alternative explanations for how the name originated. The oldest tradition assumed it went back to the beginning with Adam and Eve: 'At that time people began to call upon the name of YHWH'.[13] A later tradition traces it to the time of Moses, and links it etymologically with the Hebrew word which has been translated as 'I AM'.[14]

In demolishing the reality of the gods of other nations were the prophets not simply being chauvinistic? From today's cultural standpoint it is not easy to rescue them wholly from this charge. They do look a bit like children provocatively shouting out to other children, 'You worship only idols; our God Yahweh is the one and only true God'.

But the Israelite prophets were actually making a break with the old order of gods and replacing them with something different. This is illustrated by the radical change which took place with the Hebrew word for 'the gods" — *elohim* (plural in form). It received a new meaning and has a double use in the Old Testament. When it refers to the gods of the nations it is the plural meaning that is intended, but when it refers to the one and only god of Israel and of the world, it is to be treated as singular and it becomes a synonym for Yahweh. Thereafter the Jews fought a relentless battle against the gods, not only among other nations but also wherever they showed signs of returning among their own people. Idolatrous images were iconoclastically rejected because the one and only God was believed to be beyond all human visualization. This iconoclastic activity was carried through into Christianity and Islam.

But though visual imagery was thereafter forbidden, it was more difficult to abandon the mental imagery manifested in language. Consequently the personal language which had been freely used of the gods continued to be used of the one God. As the earlier gods had been conceived as sharing in all the human emotions and motivations, and since the values which are of ultimate concern to us humans arise out of our nature as persons, it was unthinkable that personal language would not be used in speaking of God and his ways. Of course this God could be conceived as one who possessed personal qualities magnified to an infinite degree. Accordingly, the Old Testament speaks without any embarrassment of God as being angry, repenting, changing his mind, laughing, and so on. This correlation between the personal character of God and that of humans was specifically acknowledged in the biblical affirmation — 'God created humankind in his own image or likeness'.[15] The personal language used in connection with God helped transform a word which had originated as a common noun into a proper name. God became the name of the supposed supreme supernatural Being.

Yet even while this was occurring, the usage of the term god as a common abstract noun was also retained. In biblical usage we find the word *elohim* used not only as a proper name (a synonym of Yahweh), but as a common noun related to specific people — as in 'the god of Israel', 'the god of Abraham', 'my god', 'your god'. In this usage 'god' is clearly not a personal name, but is being used in a symbolic way to refer to whatever values a person or a nation regards as supreme. This implies that if you were to ask, 'Where shall I find the god of Abraham?', the appropriate answer would be, 'Watch how Abraham lives his life and discern what he appears to regard as being his ultimate concern; that is all you will ever know of the god of Abraham. His god consists of the values he lives by and the goals he aspires to'.

In Greece the challenging of the gods took a different form. We have already noted how Xenophanes ridiculed the ancient Greek gods of Olympus. He went on to argue for a single, motionless, non-anthropomorphic god who controlled everything by the power of thought. Like the Israelite prophets, Xenophanes retained the generic use of the Greek word *theos* (god), thus enabling it to continue to perform a religious role. The later Greek philosophers followed suit, replacing the plurality of the gods as a class of super-human beings with the use of *theos* in the singular.

However, they differed in their affirmations about *theos*. Plato's *theos* was the essence of goodness, the creative source of everything, to whom was to be attributed the intelligent souls found in humans. (This has to be understood against the background of Plato's theory of 'forms' or 'universals'. The 'universals' were non-physical, abstract ideas, which, being beyond the vicissitudes of living beings and other tangible objects, are eternal. Thus Plato's *theos* was the universal, impersonal, and eternal 'form' behind the humanly conceived *theoi*, or gods of Olympus.)

For Aristotle, *theos* was even less personal than for Plato, being chiefly conceived as the Prime Mover of the cosmic system. The Stoics, in turn, conceived *theos* as the principle of rationality and order which pervaded all things. For them *theos* was the unity of all reality, so that *theos*, ether, *logos* (reason), soul of the world, and nature, were largely synonymous terms.

When Christianity broke free from Judaism and encountered Graeco-Roman culture, the influence of the Greek philosophers penetrated deeply into the Christian understanding of God. We already see Stoic influence in the prologue of St. John' Gospel:

'In the beginning was the *logos* and the *logos* was with God and the *logos* was God. He was in the beginning with God. All things came into being through him and without him there was nothing which came into being. That which came into being in him was life and the life was the light of men'.[16]

Thus, as the church departed from its Jewish matrix and lived more and more in Graeco-Roman culture, the understanding of God which the early Christians inherited from Jewish faith became synthesised with Greek philosophical thought. The God worshipped by the Jews was chiefly related to the history and fortunes of the people of Israel, as shown by the dominant place of the Exodus story in all of Israel's early traditions. Yahweh was primarily identified as the god who brought them out of Egypt, who led them into Canaan and eventually established the kingdom and dynasty of David. Thus the God of the Hebrew Bible was the 'Lord of human history' even more than he was the 'maker of heaven and earth'.

In Greek thought, however, *theos* was chiefly related to the whole universe and to nature. Plato, Aristotle, the Stoics, and the neo-Platonist mystic Plotinus (c. 205–270 C.E.) all left their mark on the way Christian theologians and other authoritative teachers through the centuries understood the nature and being of God. The transcendent, other-worldly, unchanging, and impersonal God of Plato was linked in uneasy tension with the immanent, this-worldly, history-controlling, and personal God of Israel. (The anomalous union was prevented from falling apart by the formulation of the symbolic doctrines of the Trinity and the Incarnation, to be discussed later.)

This is a very simple sketch of how the understanding of God developed in the Western cultural tradition, drawing on both Jewish and Greek traditions. From the fourth century onwards this synthetic view of God was taught authoritatively by the church, found increasingly convincing by the intelligentsia, and simply accepted by ordinary people as part and parcel of their culture. What was mostly at work in the minds of people throughout Christendom was, of course, the sense of holiness and mystery which they retained from their pre-Christian past and which they continued to find in the practices and teaching of the priesthood and church. Until the advent of the modern world, the problem faced by the authoritative hierarchy was not **un**belief but **false** belief — the belief in too many gods, spirits, and supernatural forces. (At first it had been the Christians who were regarded as atheists, because they rejected the ancestral gods — whether Greek, Roman, Teutonic, or Celtic — which people had previously worshipped.) By contrast, the reality of the one immortal and invisible God seemed to be so self-evident to all thinking people that it was quite unreasonable to deny it.

Convinced as they were that belief in the one God was perfectly consistent with common sense, theologians believed it possible to establish this belief by human reason. In the course of several centuries they developed what became known as the four proofs of the existence of God. These can be expounded in very elaborate philosophical language and a few philosophers defend these 'proofs' to this day. But the gist of these arguments can also be expressed in very simple terms, and it is at this more popular level that they still carry weight for some people. They are known as the Cosmological, Teleological, Ontological, and Moral Arguments.

The Cosmological Argument starts from the existence of the world. Since it is possible to conceive that there may have been nothing at all, it seems reasonable to infer that there must have been a reason (*logos*), cause, or creator of the world; that we call God. This inference parallels at the cosmic level what human beings are seen to do when they create tangible objects. Thus the Bible uses the image of the potter at work as a metaphorical description of God as one who can both make and also destroy what he makes.[17] Just as a pot must have a maker, so the world exists only because it has been made. The Maker of the world we call God. Because we human beings show ourselves to be rational when we make things, so the divine Maker must be a rational being, even though far beyond human intelligibility.

The Teleological Argument starts from the observation of order and design in the universe. Various organs in the human body, such as the eye for example, manifest design of breath-taking complexity. Such design does not occur by chance. Indeed, as the modern law of physics known as the second law of thermo-dynamics shows, disorder in the universe generally is always increasing. Order and design therefore point to the existence of a Cosmic Designer. That Designer we call God. This argument was used to great effect by William Paley, and his *View of the Evidences of Christianity* (1794) became a standard textbook.

The Moral Argument rests upon the universal human experience of a sense of obligation or moral duty. One of its most effective proponents in modern times was the philosopher Immanuel Kant (1724–1804). He argued that to explain satisfactorily the moral nature of the human condition, it is necessary to postulate the being of God as one who has not only made us to be morally concerned creatures, but has made this a moral universe in which worthiness is rewarded and wickedness is punished. Because we humans show moral concern, there must be a supreme moral will at work in the world and that moral will we call God.

The Ontological Argument goes back to St. Anselm (1033–1109) and sets out to show that the very concept of God implies the necessity of God's existence. Anselm defined God as 'that than which nothing greater can be conceived.' Since God, by definition, embraces all perfections, then God must exist. The argument can be set out as a simple *reductio ad absurdum* proof, as follows:

> Let God be the name of the highest reality one can conceive.
> God either exists or does not exist.
> If this God does not exist, it is possible to conceive of another God
>   who is a higher reality in that he does exist.
> But since, by definition, God is already the highest conceivable
>   reality, it is absurd to suggest a higher reality can be conceived.
> Therefore God exists.

The fallacy in this argument is that existence is not an attribute nor a perfection of the same sort as, say, goodness. Therefore, the neat logical argument of *reductio ad absurdum* collapses. Nevertheless, the argument can be expounded in such a subtle way that the fallacy becomes hidden, with the result that many intelligent people, including some philosophers, still find it convincing.

Let us now summarize the history of god. The concept originated in mythology and referred to a class of powerful but unseen beings, created by the human imagination in the ancient past to explain the mysterious phenomena of what today we call the natural world. Then came the time, in the Axial period, when these gods were rejected in favour of one basic concept to which everything else could be related. In both the Jewish and the Greek traditions the concept of 'god' was retained but underwent a distinct change in meaning and usage. What became the classical understanding of God in the Christian tradition was a synthesis of both the Jewish and Greek traditions.

It is relatively easy for us in modern times to concede that the 'gods' of pre-Axial times were the product of the collective human imagination. However, we tend to lose sight of the fact that the concept of God as found in later monotheism was simply a refinement of what originated there. The essential relationship between the 'gods' of pre-Axial times and the God of monotheism became hidden from view behind the doctrine of divine revelation which Jew, Christian, and Muslim all appealed to in defending their own unique understandings of God. Jews believe that God revealed himself and his will to Moses by the giving of the Torah. Christians believe that God revealed himself and his will through Jesus Christ. Muslims believe that God revealed his will to Muhammad through the angel Gabriel.

When the doctrine of divine revelation came under question and was either greatly modified or abandoned (as we shall discuss later), it meant that the essential continuity between the gods and God was rediscovered. Thus the term God is just as much a human creation as were the pre-Axial gods. All talk of God or of the gods is human talk.

Of course the fact that the terms were created by humans does not in itself invalidate the truth of all claims made about God. That is something else we must yet discuss. The evolution of instrumental music, for example, may have begun in the far distant past when a few cavemen after a hearty meal were pleasantly surprised by the sounds they heard when they accidentally began to knock some bones together. Such an origin does not in any way detract from the wonder of a Beethoven symphony. We have yet to discuss the value of speaking about God as a way of interpreting existence in today's world.

What we can be sure of, after this sketch of the history of God, is that all our talk of God is human talk. We humans invented it. In that sense we made the gods. And just as the first Axial Period brought 'the death of the gods', so the advent of modernity can be referred to as the beginning of the second Axial Period.[18] It is the era in which people are now speaking of the 'death of God'. To this we must turn.

Chapter Four

Has God died and, if so, why?

I n the late nineteenth century 'the death of God' was announced in a very dramatic way by Friedrich Nietzsche. He wrote a parable in which he described a madman running through the market-place with a lantern during the brightness of the morning and crying out that he was looking for God. The bystanders poked fun at him and asked him if God had lost his way or gone on a distant voyage. Thereupon he declared, 'God is dead! We have killed him'. This strange announcement silenced the onlookers and caused them to stare at him in astonishment. Thereupon the madman became silent and threw his lantern to the ground, where it broke into pieces and went out. Then he said, 'I have come too early; my time is not yet. This tremendous event is still on its way. It has not yet reached the ears of men'.

Nietzsche was drawing attention to what he took to be a very significant cultural event then occurring in Western Christendom. As we shall see in chapter 7, Nietzsche was not even the first to say 'God is dead'. Even so, as the parable conceded, he was still ahead of his time. That Nietzsche was correctly interpreting the signs of his times was confirmed one hundred years later by the eminent theologian John Macquarrie when he observed in his Gifford Lectures of 1983–1984, entitled *In Search of Deity*:

> There was a time in Western society when 'God' was an
> essential part of everyday vocabulary. The word was on everybody's
> lips . . . But in the West and among educated people throughout
> the world, this kind of God-talk has virtually ceased . . . People
> once knew, or thought they knew, what they meant when they spoke
> of God, and they spoke of him often. Now the name of god seems
> to have been retired from our everyday discourse. Even a believer, if
> he is asked 'What do you mean when you speak of God?' may find
> himself stumbling over an answer.[1]

But why has God come to have such a wide range of meanings and why (to use Macquarries's words) has 'God-talk virtually
ceased' in the public arena? It is because the idea of God as a thinking, planning, personal being, who dwells somewhere quite apart
from human beings and their world, has become unbelievable for
an increasing number of people. Apart from phrases, such as
'Thank God!', where past Christian faith has become frozen in the
language, the name of God is heard today in virtually only one
context — that is, in church circles. The church has become an
island of the past where there is spoken a language which is becoming foreign to people in the world outside. It has hardly yet dawned
upon the church that it uses a basic concept which has virtually
disappeared for common use outside the church.

Why has this happened? To understand the cultural event
to which Nietzsche was referring and which Macquarrie was
describing, we need to go back some centuries and resume the history of 'God'. A fundamental shift in human consciousness has
been reflected in language. The evidence of this shift has been
clearly observable since the Renaissance, but its roots go as far back
as the High Middle Ages.[2]

Of course, religious unbelief and scepticism are by no
means an entirely modern phenomenon. They were quite prominent features of the Axial Period, which saw the 'death of the gods'
and the rise of the great new world religions. Even as the Christian
faith was spreading through the Roman Empire, it had to defend
itself against sceptics of all kinds, such as the very able second century philosopher Celsus. He strongly criticized the miracles and
absurdities he observed in biblical history and rejected the
Christian doctrine of the Incarnation. But after the Christian
Emperor Justinian closed the pagan philosophical schools in 529

C.E., there was much less opportunity for scepticism and free rational enquiry to flourish. Such was the control exercised by the church that all criticism of Christian doctrine had to go underground. It became heresy (punishable by death and loss of eternal life) to depart from, or even question, established orthodox teaching. In the early Middle Ages Peter Lombard (1100-1160) systematized Christian doctrine into his *Four Books of Sentences* and this became the standard text of orthodox belief.

In the thirteenth century, however, Christian orthodoxy came under serious challenge when by way of Muslims in Spain the knowledge of Aristotelian philosophy reached the newly established universities of Western Christendom. In contrast with the dualist philosophy of Plato hitherto used to explore and expound Christian doctrine, Aristotle propounded a philosophy of the natural world. Whereas Plato set forth a world of ideas as the stuff of eternal reality, Aristotle turned to the physical world as the substance of reality and expounded a proto-empirical model of knowledge. This conflicted at many points with Christian orthodoxy and caused considerable turmoil among the intellectuals of the day. Since the doctrines of Christian faith were sacrosanct, a way had to be found of reconciling them with what appeared to be a convincing challenge coming from the mouth of Aristotle. The Dominican theologian Albertus (1200–1280), followed by the even more famous Thomas Aquinas (1225–1274), so successfully baptized Aristotle's natural philosophy into the Christian system of thought that Thomist teaching remained the standard for Roman Catholicism at least until Vatican II.

The Franciscan theologians, however, were never wholly satisfied with the synthesis achieved by the Dominicans, and from the former emerged the person who, perhaps more than anyone else, is the key to the modern 'death of God'. This was William of Ockham (1285–1349); he expounded what soon became known as the *Via Moderna*. He argued that only tangible objects exist and he denied that Plato's universal ideas (e.g. goodness, justice etc) had any objective reality of their own (philosophers call it their ontology). Concepts and words exist only in the human mind and they constitute the tools by which we try to understand the real world. He denied that it was possible to prove the existence of God or discover the attributes of God by human reason. The truth

51

about God (which he did not deny) had to be embraced by faith. He thus separated faith from reason.

There are two aspects of Ockham's new and quite elaborate philosophy which need to be noted in connection with the 'death of God'. The first is a methodological principle still known today as 'Ockham's razor'. This asserts that in the process of finding an explanation of phenomena one should not postulate any more entities than necessary. This means, for example, that if one can explain the occurrence of an earthquake or a brain hemorrhage through natural causes — without having to resort to God by calling one an 'act of God' and the other a 'stroke' — then one should dispense with God as a necessary cause. What has been happening increasingly in the modern world is that natural phenomena have been explained by the internal workings of the universe and God as the originating cause has become redundant.

The second point arises from the general thrust of Ockham's philosophy, which led to its being termed nominalism. Ideas and concepts are no more than names (*nomina*) created by the human mind. Ockham was one of the first to begin to see that the conceptual realm — the pattern of ideas, beliefs, theories by which we live, think, and interpret reality — is one which we ourselves have created. In the long run this would lead to the realisation that the concept of God also has been created by the collective human mind. Since Ockham remained a man of his time, however, he naturally did not see just how radical these seed-thoughts were and where they would eventually lead. Yet already Church authorities found his vigorous and critical thought so threatening that he was excommunicated and expelled from his order. By the end of the fourteenth century, however, nominalism was spreading through the universities, preparing the way for the Protestant Reformation, and helping to lay the foundations of empirical science.

Martin Luther was a nominalist. This becomes clear in his Large Catechism where he defined God as 'that to which we look for all good and where we resort in every time of need; to have a god is simply to trust and believe in one with our whole heart'. He even conceded that 'the confidence and faith of the heart alone *make* both God and an idol'.[3] Of course Luther still had confidence that divine revelation enabled one to distinguish between the true God and the false gods which the faith of the heart creates, but already he was acknowledging that the very concept of God was in part a human creation. What was to happen when the doctrine of divine revelation (to which both Ockham and Luther could appeal) also came under critical scrutiny as it did in the Enlightenment?

In the Western world, at least from the seventeenth century onwards, the belief in divine revelation came increasingly under criticism and eventually was widely rejected. The traditional understanding of God became highly vulnerable when it no longer possessed supernatural support. God had long been regarded as the proper name of a supernatural spiritual being; yet since God is neither visible nor tangible and his existence thus cannot be confirmed by any empirical method, divine revelation was absolutely necessary to establish both the reality and the attributes of God. Increasingly unable to appeal to revelation, people had no way of determining the meaning and content of the word 'God' and its signification became increasingly uncertain.

As a result, the word 'God' came to have a wide range of meanings. This is shown by a variety of terms which then came into use. The term that was coined to refer to what had become the traditional belief in God is theism. It continues to be used in academic circles and is replaced by 'monotheism' only to distinguish it from polytheism — the belief in many gods. It is primarily a philosophical term which came to be distinguished from such alternatives as deism, pantheism, panentheism, mysticism, and its polar opposite, atheism.

In **Theism** God is taken to be the name of the supernatural personal being believed to have created the world and to continue to have oversight (providence) of its affairs, intervening in them from time to time with miraculous events. Being personal, this God enters into personal relationships with humans, who are made in his image. This view of God goes far beyond what the so-called 'proofs' of the existence of God could ever establish, but theists claim that it represents what Christian faith has traditionally affirmed. So Christian orthodoxy still strongly affirms and defends theism. Evangelical Christians use it as one of the essential tests of orthodoxy by asking, "Do you believe in a personal God?"

Atheism, by its etymology, is strictly speaking the rejection of theism. The word was used in the ancient world of those who disbelieved the Greek and Roman gods, and so even the early Christians were dubbed atheists. The modern meaning of atheism emerged in the eighteenth century, and for a while it was used chiefly to describe those who did not subscribe to the orthodox Christian teaching of God. In referring to deists, pantheists and panentheists whom we have yet to mention, the term non-theist is preferable to atheist. Today the word atheist is often used by people to mean that they deny that the concept of 'God' refers to any reality at all, whether a spiritual being or simply an idea.

The understanding of God espoused by the leaders of the Enlightenment was known as **Deism**. They rejected the idea of miracles as divine or supernatural interventions into nature and they were prepared to abandon all the personal attributes ascribed to God. In other words they rejected theism. They retained the word God as the name of the creator of the universe yet did not think this God continued to be involved in the world in any personal way. Deism appealed to thinkers in the time of the rise of modern science, for it was consistent with Aristotelianism and the Cosmological Argument. Although deism is strongly rejected in theological circles it is actually very widespread at a popular level, mostly in people who have never even heard the word. When modern physicists, such as Albert Einstein, Fred Hoyle, Stephen Hawking, and Paul Davies use the term God, they are usually thinking of an infinite intelligence behind the creation of the universe; this belief is much closer to deism than to theism.

Pantheism (which by its etymology means 'everything is god') identifies God with all that exists. It regards all finite things as parts, modes, limitations, or appearances of one ultimate Being, which is all that there is. It originated with the Jewish philosopher Spinoza, who was roundly condemned by Jew and Christian. Yet it has continued to surface from time to time. Teilhard de Chardin and Paul Tillich were both accused by their critics, though unfairly so, of being pantheists.

Panentheism is a more recent term. It was coined by K.C.F. Krause (1781–1832) in the attempt to find a middle road between theism and pantheism. The former he deemed no longer convincing, and the latter too crude. Theism was thought to overemphasize the transcendence or 'otherness' of God while pantheism overemphasisd the immanence of God. Panentheism ('everything is **in** God') is the belief that the Being of God includes and penetrates the whole universe in such a way that every part of it exists in God but God is more than the universe. Although the word has hardly yet got into dictionaries, panentheism won a great deal of support among philosophers and theologians during the twentieth century. It represents the position of such people as Teilhard de Chardin, John Robinson, Paul Tillich, Jürgen Moltmann and John Macquarrie (though the last prefers the term 'dialectical theism'.[4]

Mysticism, like panentheism, has associations with both theism and pantheism. It is the belief that the only reality is one undiversified Being. In mystical thought, and in much of its practice, the multiplicity of things is ultimately repudiated. Many have dallied with mysticism, both in mediaeval and modern times, but it is generally rejected by Christian orthodoxy, which likes to affirm an unbridgeable gap between God and all he has supposedly created, including ourselves.

These various terms show, as noted above, that at least since the Enlightenment, the word 'God' came to be used with an ever wider range of meanings and this resulted in increasing uncertainty. The momentum of cultural tradition was sufficiently strong, of course, for the traditional understanding of God to prevail in the minds and experience of most people for the next two centuries. But among thinking, inquiring minds it was otherwise. The Enlightenment had set people free to think for themselves, and more and more people took the opportunity to do so. Thus the word 'God' began to fall apart, slowly at first and much more rapidly during the twentieth century, until it appeared no longer to have one clear and unambiguous meaning.

This occurred chiefly because the word 'God' has no objective referent to which we can make the same sort of public appeal as, say, to the sun. Of course it has long been acknowledged by theologians that God 'has no body', but the popular perception was otherwise. That is why Michaelangelo painted his magnificent picture of God on the ceiling of the Sistine Chapel. How did he get away with it? If the church had been faithful to its tradition that should have brought a charge of rank heresy. Paradoxically, some fifty years later the church chose to burn Bruno at the stake because he asserted, among other things, that God is not to be understood as a personal being but as the divine life permeating the whole of nature including ourselves.

So the Anglican Thirty-nine Articles begin, 'There is but one living and true God, everlasting, without body, parts or passions'. But how do we know? It is largely because the Church says so, and the Church says so because it deems itself the guardian of knowledge divinely revealed in the past; therefore it is to be believed and not questioned. One is reminded of the dictum of the Muslim theologian Malik (712–795):

> God is on the throne.
> The fact is known.
> The manner of it is unknown.
> Faith in it is necessary.
> Enquiry about it is heresy.

But once belief in divine revelation began to be questioned, as it was from the Enlightenment onwards, it was no longer sufficient for the church simply to proclaim the reality of God as true and to use its authority to enforce this belief by penalizing all who did not accept it. Even into the beginning of the twentieth century, the authority of the church and weight of peer pressure were sufficient to make people very reluctant to confess themselves openly to be atheists or even agnostics. They feared they would be ostracized as people beyond the pale.

Thus despite both his lack of perceptible form and the declining confidence in divine revelation, God remained a convincing reality for the vast majority because of his ascribed qualities and functions. The Thirty-nine Articles briefly describes him as 'of infinite power, wisdom and goodness, Maker and Preserver of all things both visible and invisible'. These qualities and functions were theologically referred to as God's attributes. Because God possesses no body, it is these attributes which really constitute the identity of God. What theologians discussed and debated through the centuries was never the being of God but the attributes of God.

Then the question arises — has God any being apart from the divine attributes? The only answer seems to be that the being of God consists of the divine attributes. God is the sum-total of the values which we humans attribute to God. Even the New Testament (perhaps unintentionally) acknowledges this when it says 'God is love'. If we take away the attributes, the term 'God' becomes an empty shell; it is rather like the algebraic 'x' waiting to be given a meaningful content from the cultural context in which the term is being used. Only then does the common noun 'god' receive a more specific connotation and become God. In short, the content of the word God has to be supplied wholly from human culture. (In the next chapter this will be illustrated by comparing the Christian God with the Muslim Allah).

Now is not the first time in the history of 'god' that this word has been emptied of meaning. As we have seen, the word 'god' originated in ancient mythology. It was coined by our ancient ancestors to refer to a class of superhuman beings, whom they visualized as controlling all the phenomena of nature and the fates of humans. Jupiter, Venus, Marduk, Asherah and all the rest were conceived as the names of personal entities that could be honoured by sacrificial offerings, addressed in prayer, and even coaxed to show favour to the worshipper. The prophets of Israel denied that these gods had any real existence; they had no ontological reality. These gods were humanly created and should not be worshipped. This meant that the class of beings referred to as the gods existed only in the human mind; to worship them as objective beings was an act of idolatry.

As the Israelite prophets may be said to have demytholo-gized ' the gods' in the first Axial Period, so this second Axial Period has led to the 'demythologizing' of 'God'. Although the Israelites pioneered a new way of using god-language in that 'God' had to be associated with a human to have any real content (as described in the last chapter), the word God soon became objecti-fied and treated as the proper name of a supernatural spiritual being. This can be illustrated from the Bible. In the earliest story of creation (Genesis 2–3) the word God is still associated with the proper name YHWH as 'the YHWH God'. But in the later story of origins (Genesis 1) the proper name YHWH is dropped and 'God' is used as including the content of the more personal YHWH. In Israelite tradition itself, therefore, God came to be spoken about, personally addressed in prayer, and even coaxed to favour Israel, in much the same way as Jupiter, Venus and Marduk had been in pre-Axial times. It was in this way that the brave new start made by the Israelites in speaking about God in a new way gradually reverted to something nearer the pre-Axial usage. In a similar way we find that, as Buddhism spread and became synthesized with other cultures, the 'gods' began to reappear under different names in popular Buddhism.

To treat God as the name of a supernatural being, even though regarded as 'the Supreme Being', is to revert to the usage which the Israelite prophets had begun to abandon. As the class of beings called 'gods' had been a human construct, so the word 'God' is also a humanly created concept. As the Israelites retained the word 'God' but began to use it in a new way, so if we retain the word 'God' after the second Axial Period, then we have to learn to speak about God in a radically new way. But this may be difficult to achieve.

The Second Axial Period leaves us with a variety of choices just as the first one did. In the first Axial Period the Buddhists opted to abandon god-talk altogether, while the Middle Eastern traditions chose to retain the term 'god' and to use it in a new way. So also today we have the choice of abandoning god-talk altogether. This course of action is strongly advised by atheists and secular humanists on the grounds that in western culture the assumption that God is the name of the Supreme Being has been so dominant, and remains so intrinsically part of the traditional church, that there is no practical possibility of 'learning to speak of God in a radically new way'. This option affirms not only that God is dead but that god-talk also is becoming obsolete. The observation by Macquarrie quoted earlier suggests that western society generally has already taken this option.

There are others who in varying degrees accept that God is dead in the sense that 'God' can no longer mean what it meant in the past but who regard the term as so important that we cannot do without it. Paul Tillich, perhaps the most creative theologian of the twentieth century, tried to rescue God-talk by speaking of God as 'being-itself' or 'ground of being'. By this phrase he meant that God is the unconditional reality upon which all existing things depend for their being and, to this end, he treated 'being' as a verb rather than as a noun. Even though this way of talking avoids the implication that God is the name of a supernatural being separate from the physical universe, it is far from clear just what 'being itself' is. One has the feeling of being tricked by linguistic sleight of hand.

Tillich fully acknowledged that 'God' is a symbolic term and can be talked about only in language which is symbolic and metaphorical. This means that all talk about God is of necessity inadequate. Setting too much store on any particular word or description quickly slides into idolatry. Even Tillich was forced in the end to resort to such terms as 'the God beyond God'.

Tillich made the creative suggestion that 'God' is a symbolic term by which we refer to whatever concerns us in an ultimate way. He said 'the fundamental symbol of our ultimate concern is God'.[5] Such a view has much to be said for it. It actually continues the usage begun by Israelites who spoke of 'the God of Abraham', 'the God of Israel' and, later, 'the God of Jesus Christ'.

Even Tillich, however, was reluctant to surrender the last element of objectivity in the concept of God. It was left to the more radical theologian Don Cupitt to take this step, which he did in *Taking Leave of God* (1981). Here he speaks of God as 'the mythical embodiment of all that one is concerned with in the spiritual life'.[6] He refers to this way of speaking as a 'non-realist' view of God. Whereas the realist or traditional view of God imagines God to be an objective being, the non-realist treats all god-talk as a symbolic language which, though originating in ancient mythology, may still be found useful in order to refer to the highest ideals, values, and aspirations to which we feel obliged to give our allegiance. Strangely enough it is closely parallel to the initial premise of the Ontological argument — 'Let God be the name of the highest reality one can conceive'.

The term 'non-realist' roughly means 'having no objective reality'; it has a long philosophical history and goes back at least to the medieval nominalists, originating with William of Ockham and continuing through Martin Luther and Ludwig Feuerbach. Still, however attractive and useful this approach to god-talk may be, it accepts the fact that God who was imaged as a supernatural, personal being has died.

Can Christianity survive without this image of God? All traditional and orthodox Christians answer with a resounding 'No!'

Even Nietzsche did so! 'Christianity is a system, a consistently thought out and *complete* view of things', he said. 'If one breaks out of it a fundamental idea, the belief in God, one thereby breaks the whole thing to pieces: one has nothing of any consequence left in one's hands.'[7] Yet when Nietzsche wrote those words he was assuming the specific understanding of God which is properly called theism.

What has died is the theistic image of God as a personal divine Creator. Moreover, theism began to be questioned in the seventeenth century, the very time when this word was first coming into common use in order counter such alternative terms as deism and pantheism. It is amusing that we even find the term theism being rejected at that time by some devout Christians. The celebrated chemist and natural philosopher Robert Boyle (1627–1691), who had been a strong advocate of the propagation of Christianity in India, left a bequest to found the Boyle lectures: these were intended to 'prove the Christian religion against all notorious Infidels, to wit, Atheists, **Theists**, Pagans, Jews, and Mahometans'.[8]

Presently I shall try to show that theism does not properly belong to Christianity anyway. This term came into common use at the onset of the Second Axial Period simply because something was going seriously wrong with the orthodox understanding of God. The Christian understanding of God, from at least the fifth century onwards, was not theism but trinitarianism. To this we shall now turn.

Chapter Five

Why did Christians invent the Holy Trinity?

o suggest that Christians invented the Holy Trinity may sound quite shocking — until we start to think about it. Living, as we do, on this side of the second Axial Period we are in a better position to understand how human languages, cultures, and religious doctrines have evolved and developed over long periods. They are still evolving; they do so in tiny increments — whenever we have a new experience, create a new idea we want to share with others, and invent a new word to express it. All languages, concepts, and doctrines are human inventions.

Up until only about two hundred years ago, however, it seemed self-evident to nearly everybody that languages went back to the beginning of time and were of divine or supernatural origin. We can now see that language and culture are human products. Similarly it was long believed that Christian doctrines, such as that of the Holy Trinity, were divinely revealed. We can now say that our Christian forbears invented them. They were not aware that they were inventing them, for language, culture, and religious ideas evolved slowly.

We now know that religious doctrines have a history from the time they first take shape in people's minds until they are subsequently enunciated in more permanent and generally acceptable forms. The Christian doctrine of the Holy Trinity, as we shall see, had just such a history and it took some four hundred years to reach its classical form. That is why we can unequivocally assert that it was invented — invented by Christians to express their faith.

To understand the invention of the Holy Trinity we need to see it within the larger context of the whole history of God, as sketched in chapter 3. There we observed that god-talk is a language which humans invented in the far distant past in order to make some sense of life. It was in the course of the two Axial Periods, however, that god-talk went through crises and was subjected to radical changes of usage. As we have already observed in chapter 3, it was during the first Axial Period that the gods were at last acknowledged for what they were — human creations. In modern jargon we may say that the mythical spiritual beings known as the gods were demythologized. This caused the concept of god to fall out of use in some places, as in the Buddhist and Confucian cultures. In other places, such as Israel, Greece, and Arabia, the traditional word 'god' was retained but supplied with a new content and usage.

When Muhammad, for example, as a consequence of his revelatory experience, tried to shift the allegiance of his fellow Arabs away from the non-existent gods they had previously worshipped, to whom or what should he point them? He was led to invent a new term — Allah. This word is made up of the ordinary Arabic word for a god — *ilah* — preceded by the definite article, *al*. Allah literally means '**The** god', namely the only true god. The Shahada (the basic Islamic confession of faith) declares 'There is no god but *the* God'; it starts with the rejection of the gods and then goes on to the affirmation of Allah.

Of course, Muhammad did not **consciously** invent the new usage; he declared, and all Muslims sincerely believe, that this term was revealed to him by Allah himself when he encountered Gabriel at the time of his initial experiences. Only non-Muslims, looking on from outside the Islamic world, are in a position to suggest that Muhammad's creative unconscious (to use Jungian terminology) invented a new usage for the 'god' word, even if he was unaware it did so.

What had taken place among the Israelites more than a thousand years before was more complicated than that. The

Israelites had retained for their own god the proper name YHWH and frequently used it in association with the Hebrew word for God (*elohim*), as in the phrase 'YHWH the god of Israel'. As time went on, however (as already noted in the previous chapter), it became common for the term *elohim* to be used by itself as a synonym for YHWH. In the post-exilic period the term *elohim* was used more and more frequently and YHWH ceased to be pronounced at all, for fear of breaking the third commandment, which forbade the taking the name of YHWH in vain. In this way the Hebrew word *elohim* came to be used as if it were a proper name, just as the literal meaning of Allah came to be forgotten and the word used as if were a proper name. Similarly in the English language 'God' has long been treated as a proper name, though philosophers debate the legitimacy of this.

The use of the word God as if it were a proper name has led to many difficulties, for the meaning of 'God' can vary greatly from culture to culture. When we examine the ways Christians, Jews, and Muslims think about God we find there are some very significant differences. For Jews, God is the One who led the Jewish people out of Egypt, gave them the Torah on Mt. Sinai, and is today opening the way for their return to the Land of Promise. For Christians, God is the One who became incarnate in Jesus Christ and, through him, founded the institution of the church. For Muslims, God is the One who sent Muhammad to be the last of the prophets and who delivered to him the Qur'an. These are very different statements about God and are in serious conflict at a number of vital points.

Because Jews, Christians, and Muslims are all monotheists who assert that there is only one God, there has been a tendency to assume that they all believe in the same God, yet in different ways. But is it the same God? If the only way to define the meaning of the word 'God' is by means of the attributes associated with it, and these attributes show significant differences, then it can hardly be claimed to be the same God. There is one basic attribute, however, which is common to all three and that is the function God was believed to perform as the Creator of the world and of all living creatures. (This also, incidentally, is the one divine function which is common to theism, deism, panentheism, and pantheism.)

The fact that there is at least one divine attribute common to all meanings has prompted some to explain the diversity of belief, even within monotheism, by arguing that they are all inadequate descriptions of the same hidden reality. In practice this usually means that one regards one's own tradition as the true understanding of God and all others as belief systems which are partly true and partly false. Such an argument is open to the devastating criticism of being arbitrarily chauvinistic. Furthermore, it acknowledges that some views of God can be seriously mistaken. If that is so, how can we be sure they are not all astray? This is what the French humanist Montaigne (1533–1592) pointed out when the sharp division between Protestant and Catholic made him realise how much our beliefs are shaped by the cultural environment in which we are reared.

And how did this cultural environment arise? It evolved as the glacially slow creation of our forbears. Since languages and cultures have all been humanly invented, it is not surprising that there are different languages, different cultures, different ways of interpreting life, different ways of being religious, and different ways of using god-talk. Jew, Christian and Muslim, in spite of all claiming to be monotheists, do not worship the same God in view of the fact that they conceive of God differently.

Christians, in particular, are not monotheists in the way Jews and Muslims are, for the historical reason that they radically modified monotheism during the early centuries and replaced it with trinitarianism. This was when they invented the terminology of the Holy Trinity and, in doing so, abandoned the Jewish theism of primitive Christianity. Most of those who have been defending theism since the sixteenth century onwards seem to have overlooked or ignored the doctrine of the Holy Trinity. Much of what they say is directed towards theism rather than trinitarianism. In theism God is conceived as the supreme divine Creator who is entirely separate from what has been created. There is an unbridgeable gulf between the theistic God and all that has been created. Yet this is exactly what the doctrine of the Holy Trinity controverts, for it asserts that the gulf has been bridged.

We must now explore this doctrine for, while it may be outmoded in its traditional form, the reasons which lay behind its invention may help us understand why the modern secular world emerged out of the Christian West and not, say, out of the Islamic world, the Hindu world, or the Chinese world.

Most Christians today are prepared to confess that they do not understand the doctrine of the Holy Trinity. Many of them declare it a holy mystery and so evade the problem. On the other hand, those who think they do understand the doctrine of the Holy Trinity usually get it wrong by falling into one of the ancient heresies. The doctrine of the Holy Trinity may be compared with what the Chinese classic *Tao Te Ching* says of the Tao (Way):

> He who speaks does not know,
> And he who knows does not speak,

There is a story of a theological student who was so delighted by the lecture he heard on the Holy Trinity that he jumped up to thank the lecturer. 'Thank you, sir' he said excitedly, 'you put it so clearly. I have never before been able to understand the doctrine of the Trinity as I do now'. The lecturer sighed deeply, 'If you understand it as clearly as that, I shall have to start and explain it all over again'.

It is doubtful if the doctrine of the Holy Trinity was ever meant to be understood and certainly not in the way we explain and understand everyday phenomena. Those who think it tells us something about the nature of a theistic God have certainly got it wrong. The Holy Trinity is essentially a formula. It was invented by Christians of the first four or five centuries for the purpose of affirming and safeguarding certain basic experiences. We even know the name of the man in whose writings the term Trinity is first found. He was a Roman lawyer named Tertullian (160-200 C.E.). But the seeds of the doctrine were sown much earlier and it was to be a further two centuries after him before it received full authorisation.

When Christians try to defend a pure theism today they usually, though unconsciously, focus on the Father Creator and identify the Father alone with God. It is true that the very first followers of Jesus were theists, as is shown by the Lord's prayer, which encourages us to pray to 'Our Father who is in heaven'. This **is** a theistic prayer because it is a Jewish prayer, formulated before the doctrine of the Holy Trinity was put together. Jesus was a theist and not a trinitarian. He was a theist simply because theism was part of the Jewish culture which shaped Jesus. Jesus was not a trinitarian because Jesus was a Jew and not a Christian; trinitarian Christianity evolved only after his death.

Even the first generation of Christians, led by James and Peter, remained Jewish and were not trinitarians but theists. They lived in Jerusalem, went to the Temple, and observed the Jewish laws. They still saw Jesus through Jewish eyes. In their view Jesus remained fully human like themselves. They denied the later story of the virgin birth and the growing belief in the divinity of Jesus, claiming simply that he was the Messiah, a role intended for a descendant of King David. After his death he had been taken to heaven in glory and from there he would return to restore the Kingdom of Israel. In the Epistle of James we may have the best New Testament example of their thinking. They were rejected by the Jews because they affirmed Jesus to be the Messiah, and they were eventually cold-shouldered and rejected by the Gentile Christians because they did not accept Jesus as divine. We hear no more of them after the fifth century.

It was Gentile Christianity which developed the doctrine of the Holy Trinity. The earliest hint of it is to be found in the writings of Paul in the words which have become widely known as a Christian benediction — 'The grace of the Lord Jesus Christ, the love of God and the fellowship of the Holy Spirit be with you all'.[1] It is not yet a trinity but rather a triad of experiences which are here brought together in close association: the experience of the inspiring grace of Jesus (mediated through the apostles), the experience of the love of God (inherited from the Jews), and the experience of spiritual empowerment received in the Christian community.

Some thirty years later, when Matthew's Gospel was written, we find the same three elements occurring together in what was becoming the standard baptismal formula — 'baptizing them in the name of the Father and of the Son and of the Holy Spirit'.[2] It was by being baptized in this three-fold name that people were incorporated into the Christian community to become members of the body of Christ. In the ancient world names were thought to convey something of the essence or quality of a person; they were not just labels for handy reference, as they are for us. That is why the Jews thought it to be sacrilegious to utter the name of YHWH carelessly. To be baptized in the name of the Father and of the Son and of the Holy Spirit was to pass through the doorway which led to the triad of experiences described in the benediction noted above.

As Christians began to reflect on this triad, they slowly developed the formula of the Holy Trinity. By the end of the second century it was being spelled out by Irenaeus (c. 130–200 C.E.) as follows:

> This is the order of the rule of faith. The first point is this — God the Father, not made, not material, invisible: one God creator of all things. The second point is this: the Word of God, Son of God, Jesus Christ our Lord, who at the end of the age was made man, visible and tangible in order to abolish death and show forth life and produce perfect reconciliation between God and man. And the third point is this: the Holy Spirit, through whom the prophets prophesied, who at the end of the age was poured out in a new way upon humankind.[3]

What this developing triad of focal points achieved was to keep in close association the three areas of faith and experience which Christians regarded as being of highest importance. What we have to keep in mind, however, is that they had no idea of how Christians of later centuries would draw upon their words and give them an absolute authority that had not been intended. This was a very fluid stage in the evolving Christian movement. The New Testament, though now written, had not yet been officially declared to be Holy Scripture in the way the Jewish Bible was. Paul and his successors felt quite free to express just what they thought and felt at the time. In this process, however, what was intended to be tentative but helpful, exploratory thought gradually assumed the status of authority. Much of the later construction of the doctrine of the Holy Trinity depended on the exact words used; Paul's letters and the Gospels were pored over and interpreted as if they contained the revelation of divine information.

The eventual authority bestowed on the early Christian writings when they were given the status of Holy Scripture led to much unjustified theological speculation in the early centuries. One is reminded of the story of a senior bishop who said that what worried him about the church was that ideas which had been quite innovative when he was a student had come by the end of his life to possess apostolic authority.

Now it is one thing to keep three areas of experience in loose association, without defining too closely just how they are related. It is quite another when enquiring critical minds try to plumb the depths of these relationships, for then acute problems are likely to arise That is exactly what happened in the next three centuries after Irenaeus.

People were not satisfied simply with making three points or baptizing in the three-fold name. What started as a triad of experiences eventually became a new way of understanding God and one quite distinctive of the Christian tradition. The Creeds were expounded in a trinitarian form and all subsequent confessions followed the pattern. By way of example, let us look at The thirty-nine Articles of the Anglican Communion. It starts off:

> There is but one living and true God, everlasting, without body, parts or passions; of infinite power, wisdom and goodness; the Maker and Preserver of all things visible and invisible.

That is theism, pure and simple, though rather more Greek than Jewish. But the Confession does not stop there; it goes on:

> And in unity of this Godhead there be three Persons, of one substance, power and eternity, the Father, the Son and the Holy Ghost.

We should notice the subtle change, from 'God' to 'Godhead'. There is a bit of sleight of hand going on here. What has just been said about God (as if in being a Maker and Preserver, God is a personal being) does not fit quite so well with what is now said about the Godhead. If we ask what is meant by 'the Godhead' we find that it is not so much **a being** as **a quality** — godhood, the quality of being divine.

The effect of this subtle change from God to Godhead has the effect of fudging the transition now taking place from theism to something else. Pure theism is now being transformed into trinitarianism. The Christian view of God is not belief in one divine creator, full stop. (That would be theism!) The Christian view of

God is of the Father, the Son and the Holy Spirit in one Godhead or, as stated above, 'three Persons, of one substance, power and eternity'.

Now these are words which today simply lead to a lot of misunderstanding. Behind them lie three to four centuries of fierce theological debate carried on in Greek philosophical terms which we find rather foreign to our thinking in today's secular world. On the one hand, they wanted to affirm the unity of God, received from their Jewish heritage and confirmed in the philosophies of Plato and Aristotle. On the other hand, they wanted to find places in this one God, not only for divine creativity but also for everything they had received from Jesus Christ and from their experience of empowerment in the Christian community.

They began to use two Greek words which are difficult to translate. The first is *hypostasis*. This has a variety of meanings in Greek and so it is a somewhat slippery and ambiguous term to begin with. It led to a great deal of confusion even in the ancient world, especially when they came to translate the word into Latin. The word *hypostasis* is already found a number of times in the New Testament, where it is variously translated as 'foundation', 'substance', 'steadiness', 'confidence'.

The second word was *ousia*. This ought to be easier to understand for it is derived from the common Greek verb meaning 'to be' and can be translated as 'being', 'essence', 'true nature of something'. Yet it also had another meaning and could be used to refer to 'one's property' or 'substance'. The word is found only twice in the New Testament, and there it is used to refer to the property given by the father to the prodigal son, who later squandered it. So the ancient theologians could hardly have chosen two more ambiguous words with which to invent their doctrine of the Holy Trinity, particularly since *hypostasis* and *ousia* were once regarded as synonyms. It is hardly surprising that theologians fought like cat and dog over these terms.

So the Greeks finally described the Holy Trinity of Father, Son and Holy Spirit as three '*hypostases*' in one '*ousia*'. But how were the Roman theologians to find equivalents in Latin to these already slippery terms? Whereas the Greek theologians were known for their philosophical expertise, the forte of the Roman mind was law. It was the acute legal mind of Tertullian, which was chiefly responsible for the formulation of the Holy Trinity as expounded in the Latin language, and subsequently for Western Christendom.

There was another Greek term already being used in the developing doctrine of the Trinity. It was the word *prosopon*, which means 'face' or 'countenance'. It is this word rather than the word 'hypostasis' which lies behind the Latin word *persona* chosen by Tertullian. This Latin term referred to the mask which an actor wore on the stage to indicate the role he was playing. This is a much easier term to understand than *hypostasis*; though if translated as 'face', it had the disadvantage of implying that God could be seen, and this would controvert the inheritance from Jewish thought that God can never be seen. But if translated as 'role' it certainly makes good sense, indicating that though God is one, God plays three different roles. However, to treat the term persona as equivalent to our word 'person' is very misleading.

Now when Tertullian came to look for an equivalent of *ousia* he chose the word *substantia*. In some respects this is very odd, for *substantia* is a literal translation into Latin of the Greek *hypostasis*, both words being derived in their respective languages from roots meaning 'to stand under'. So whereas the Greek theologians described the Holy Trinity of Father, Son and Holy Spirit as 'three *hypostaseis* in one *ousia*' the Latin theologians spoke of 'three *personae* in one *substantia*". It is from this latter phrase that there has come into English the well-known 'three persons in one substance', found in the Thirty-Nine Articles and other Confessions.

This is a brief and very simplistic sketch of how Christians invented the Holy Trinity. It would take a whole library to hold all that was written, both in the ancient world and since, about this extraordinary new doctrine. From no later than the fifth century it has been official Christian teaching that God is at the same time both three and one. If God had been up there in his high heaven, he would have had a good laugh at all the verbal gymnastics which went on in these human attempts to penetrate the secret of his divine being.

How did Christians come to arrive at a formula which, on the face of it, is a mathematical contradiction? The answer lies in another Christian doctrine which was developing at the same time.

This is the doctrine of the Incarnation or enfleshment of the divine in the human condition. In order to incorporate the doctrine of the Incarnation, the theism inherited from the Jewish path of faith — which affirms a great gulf between God the Creator and humankind — had to be transformed into trinitarianism. In doing so, the unity of God was turned into a divine relationship of Father, Son, and Holy Spirit — a relationship which effectively bridged the gulf between God and humanity.

To the doctrine of the Incarnation we must now turn. First we shall trace the way in which the human Jesus came to be regarded as divine. Then we shall observe how expressing this as the incarnation of God meant that whatever could be conceived as the divine reality was being enfleshed in the human condition. It will then be argued that the twin doctrines of the Incarnation and of the Holy Trinity indirectly led to the modern secular world. The replacement of theism by trinitarianism was destined to spell the end of theism. We have now taken the first step in the attempt to show that Christianity is not really wedded to theism.

Chapter Six

How did Jesus become God?

n 1974 a Roman Catholic scholar called Peter de Rosa published a book called *Jesus who Became Christ*. Not long before that, after an impressive academic career, de Rosa had been dismissed as Vice-Principal of Corpus Christi College, London. That was a college for training Catholic teachers, which the Catholic Church closed down because it was becoming too radical. We shall begin with the question Peter de Rosa set out to answer — How did Jesus become Christ? — for this is where one must start in answering the question of how Jesus became God.

Until modern times no one asked how Jesus became the Christ for the simple reason that, once the end of the process had been reached, it was then read back into the beginning. In classical Christian teaching Jesus had always been the Christ. Indeed, the question had actually been turned the other way round: at issue was not how Jesus had become Christ but how the eternal Word of God (Christ) had become Jesus. John's Gospel put it this way: 'And the Word became flesh and dwelt among us and we beheld his glory . . . full of grace and truth'.[1] It is from this verse, and this verse only, that the seminal term incarnation is derived.

Thus Jesus was believed to have been the Christ from the very moment of his conception in the womb of his mother Mary.

As Christians read the Gospels all through later history and right up until modern times, everything attributed to Jesus could also be said of the Christ. Though the term 'Christ' originated as a title (being the Greek translation of the Hebrew term Messiah, or 'anointed one'), it came to be treated as a proper name. 'Jesus', 'Jesus Christ', 'Christ' were all synonyms for the same person. It was not until the revolution in biblical studies which originated in the nineteenth century that it became necessary to separate Jesus of Nazareth from the Christ figure.[2] It was this separation which then raised the question of how Jesus became the Christ.

We shall now sketch how the historical Jesus of Nazareth became the heavenly Christ. It is not an account of public events of the kind we could put together to show how a citizen, by a succession of steps, finally became a modern day President. Messiahship was not a public office to which a person could be elected or appointed at some specific time and the occurrence recorded as an historical event. Any account of how Jesus became Christ has to be one which shows how the beliefs about Jesus developed and grew in the minds of his followers both during and after his lifetime. The Christian proclamation of Jesus as the Christ originated as a subjective evaluation of the role of Jesus by his followers. Later generations tended to interpret these subjective affirmations as if they had been objective events, thus giving them a public and historical character they had never possessed.

The first part of this story is well documented in the New Testament and it became very clear as soon as scholars began, about two hundred years ago, to read the Bible historically. Until then the Bible had been read as if it had all been written on one level and by the same author, namely God. That meant that there could be no inconsistencies; any apparent contradictions were attributed to faulty interpretation on the part of the reader. As we noted in chapter 1, the various books of the Bible were written by different people at different times and reflected different historical contexts and viewpoints; the acknowledgement of this by scholars brought to light the evident diversity.

In particular it came to be realised that the Gospels were written neither by apostles nor by eye-witnesses of what they recounted. It is now widely acknowledged that the Gospels were written in the period 70–100 C.E. being derived partly from collections of stories circulating in oral tradition, and partly from the creative inspiration of the evangelist in question. This revolution in biblical study had the effect of dramatically changing our understanding of Jesus as the Christ. The traditional belief that Jesus was the Christ from the beginning was now replaced by a surprising variety of conflicting answers to the question of how Jesus became the Christ.

Within the body of stories handed down by oral tradition we find a surprising variety of subjective judgements as to when and how Jesus was first believed to be the Christ. Some of these proclamations sound as if they are reporting objective events, but their subjective character is confirmed by the fact that several different accounts appear at various points in the New Testament. We should further note that these 'objective events' fall into the category of 'acts of God'. Anything judged by humans to be 'an act of God', either in ancient or modern times, belongs to the category of human judgement or interpretation and not to the category of historical event. The historian can investigate a public event but can neither confirm nor deny the claim that it is an 'act of God'.

By far the most significant proclamation of an 'act of God' in the New Testament is the assertion that God raised Jesus from the dead. As this shall presently be noted as the basis for the affirmation of Jesus as the Christ, and as traditional Christians today tend to regard the Gospel stories relating to the resurrection of Jesus as incontrovertible proof that Jesus is the divine Son of God, we need to look at these narratives first.[3]

How did Christians come to believe that the crucified Jesus was raised from the dead? The traditional answer is quite clear. The narratives in the Gospels and Acts seem to affirm very clearly that on the third day after his death on the cross Jesus rose from the dead in a renewed or glorified body, showed himself to his disciples over a period of forty days, and then ascended into heaven.

We may call this the assumed 'objective account' of the resurrection of Jesus. It was generally accepted as factual by Christians from about the end of the first century until a little over 200 years ago. But when the New Testament narratives began to be studied historically as independent stories and placed in their historical contexts by later editors, a quite different understanding of the resurrection of Jesus from the dead came to light.

David Strauss, in 1843, was the first to argue that certain stories about Jesus in the New Testament are more properly to be treated as myths, or symbolic stories, particularly when they narrate how God spoke or acted. He contended that these arose in the early church and were grounded on motifs already extant in the Old Testament. For the account of the Ascension of Jesus into heaven, for example, there was already a clear precedent in the Old Testament story of Elijah's ascension into heaven in a whirlwind.[4] (Incidentally, this story also provides the prototype for the pentecostal outpouring of the Spirit following the ascension of Jesus, for a double share of Elijah's spirit is what Elisha is said to have asked for, and to have received, after the ascension of Elijah.)

There is now widespread agreement, that the story of the ascension is a mythical account and not an historical event. The reason for this concession is obvious. While it had made very good sense when taken at face value in the world-view shared by the ancients and the mediaevalists, it makes no sense at all in the world-view we share today. To assert that the risen body of Jesus ascended into some special heaven above the earth is to turn the story into a ridiculous piece of space science fiction. Consequently, of the traditional account of what happened to Jesus after his death, this was the first element to be demythologised — that is, interpreted symbolically rather than taken at face value.

But while the narrative of the ascension of Jesus into heaven is undoubtedly late in its present form, the idea which gave rise to it is quite early and may well have been the very beginning of the resurrection tradition, rather than its end result. That idea was the glorification of the crucified Jesus. As we shall presently see, the belief that Jesus was the Messiah developed after his death and then was read back ever earlier; similarly, the Easter faith may well have begun with a vision of the glorification of the crucified Jesus. We have just such a vision attributed to Stephen before his martyrdom.

> He looked to heaven and saw the glory of God and Jesus standing at the right hand of God and he said, 'Behold, I see the heavens opened and the Son of man standing at the right hand of God'.[5]

It has been suggested that the story of the Transfiguration of Jesus does not belong chronologically within the ministry of

Jesus, where Mark's Gospel has mistakenly placed it — an error copied and thus compounded by those of Matthew and Luke. Rather, it originated as an early glorification vision which later sparked the resurrection stories. This suggestion has been supported by such internationally acclaimed scholars as Heinrich Meyer (1800–1873), Julius Wellhausen (1844–1918), Adolf Harnack (1851–1930), Alfred Loisy (1857–1940), Maurice Goguel (1880–1955) and Rudolf Bultmann (1884–1976).

It is generally agreed, with Gospel record support, that when Jesus was crucified the disciples deserted him and fled. They returned to Galilee greatly dispirited, suffering acute anxiety and bewilderment, and wondering why God allowed a man of such quality and power to come to such a tragic end. Those are the very conditions under which the unconscious depths of the human psyche can prove to be extraordinarily creative. The psyche, drawing upon both remembered experience and the basic symbols already embedded there, creates a vision which resolves the issue.[6]

Here then were Jewish disciples whose minds, like that of Elijah in his time of crisis, turned back to Sinai, the source of their faith. In the vision created by the unconscious (possibly of Peter), he and his two closest companions James and John, were led back by the memory of their Master to climb, in imagination, that same high mountain. This is the story as Mark tells it:

> And Jesus was transfigured before them, and his garments became glistening, intensely white . . . And there appeared to them Elijah with Moses; and they were talking to Jesus . . . And a cloud overshadowed them, and a voice came out of the cloud, 'This is my beloved son; listen to him'. And suddenly looking around they no longer saw anyone but Jesus only.[7]

There are some very significant elements in this vision, very like those which were already present in Jewish tradition:

1. When Moses went up Mt Sinai the glory of the Lord enveloped it in a cloud, and when he went down his face glistened.
2. Elijah is said not to have died but to have been taken to heaven in a whirlwind.
3. Though Moses had died and been buried, a late Jewish legend told how Moses had been taken by God into heaven.[8]
4. Moses and Elijah were thus the only two Israelites believed by Jews to be already with God in heaven.

These ingredients from the Jewish tradition, coupled with the bewilderment of the disciples, supplied ample raw material for an apostolic vision. Above all else the vision affirmed that the death of Jesus was not a meaningless tragedy. It showed that Jesus had been placed by God on a level with Moses and Elijah. The glistening or transfiguration demonstrated symbolically that Jesus had been glorified.

The Easter faith probably arose from visions of the exaltation of the crucified Jesus to the heavenly presence along with Moses and Elijah. C. F. Evans raised the possibility that, 'the concept of the exaltation to the right hand of god . . . was prior to the idea of resurrection in establishing belief in Jesus' lordship and messiahship, for it leads directly to it, while resurrection from the dead, as such, does not'.[9]

But such is the nature of the enquiring human mind that it was not sufficient for the ongoing Christian community just to say that the glorified Jesus had been seen in visions. Paul tells us that Peter was the first to see the glorified Jesus, yet no report of this vision has survived. This is possibly because it was surpassed by what seemed to be the more convincing stories which were told later. As soon as Christians were convinced that some had received visions of the exaltation of Jesus, and since they knew for certain he had been crucified and gone to the abode of the dead, then it followed that he must have risen from the dead. So the earliest Christian records declare that Jesus had been raised from the dead. At first this was chiefly a synonym for exaltation, for resurrection certainly did not mean the return to life in this world. And yet, during the last third of the first century, several stories began to emerge which seemed to imply just that. In John 21 we are even told of Jesus breakfasting with the disciples after their catch of fish.

There is widespread agreement among biblical scholars that the Easter faith arose in Galilee; but as Christian imagination turned from initial visions of Jesus in glory to stories of his appearing on earth, attention began to shift back to Jerusalem. It was assumed that his body must have been buried in a tomb and in that case the tomb must now be empty. So a story arose of how the tomb was found empty by some women. The key to that story is the angel or mystery man robed in white who said, 'The crucified Jesus whom you seek is not here, for he has risen'.[10] The words spoken by the angel are the foundation stone on which the story was built; the conviction that Jesus was risen led to the story of the empty tomb and not the other way round.

Because the empty tomb stories have long dominated the tradition, they shape our imagination when we hear the term 'rising from the dead'. When this term was first used, however, it did not refer to someone coming out of a tomb. It referred to the rising from Sheol, the abode of the dead, and the ascension into heaven. This is still reflected in the Johannine story of Mary Magdalene, where Jesus says, 'Don't touch me, for I am ascending to my father'.[11] Viewed from the standpoint of today's cosmology it sounds rather amusing: Jesus was on his journey from the underworld of the dead to the heavenly world above when Mary accidentally met him on the way and was in danger of impeding his progress.

As the stories progressed, the risen Christ came to be described in more and more physical terms. It is on the basis of these late resurrection stories that conservative Christians today defend what they call 'the bodily resurrection'. But when we trace the glorification and resurrection of Jesus back to visions, we find that we are dealing with a subjective process rather than an objective one. The Christian affirmation that Jesus had been raised from the dead did not refer to something which happened objectively to the body of Jesus; it reflected a subjective process taking place in the minds and hearts of the followers of Jesus. Thus, what was originally a visionary experience assumed the character of an historical event. As we are now about to see, faith in the resurrection (or exaltation) of Jesus and the acknowledgement of Jesus as the Messiah (Christ) are so closely connected as to be substantially the same. As Rudolf Bultmann said, 'The resurrection is nothing else than the rise of faith in the risen Lord. . . . Faith in the resurrection is really the same thing as faith in the saving efficacy of the cross'.[12]

The New Testament is our chief source for understanding the rise of Christianity. It still remains a treasury of invaluable documents, but in the aftermath of the revolution in biblical studies, the several accounts of how Jesus became the Christ are noticeably different. Here are some of the more significant clues:

A. In Acts 2 we find the following words put into the mouth of Peter:

> Men of Israel, hear these words: Jesus of Nazareth, a man attested to
> you by God with mighty works and wonders and signs which God
> did through him in your midst . . . you crucified and killed by the
> hands of lawless men . . . **This Jesus God raised up**, and of that
> we are all witnesses . . . Let all the house of Israel know assuredly
> that **God has made him both Lord and Christ, this Jesus whom
> you crucified**.

We do not know whether these words genuinely came
from Peter or (and this is more likely) from later oral tradition. But
whoever first uttered those words was proclaiming his belief that it
was through God's act of raising Jesus from the dead that Jesus
became the Christ. In other words, on this view, the man Jesus
became the Christ at some point after his death on the cross.
Something similar is implied by Paul when, in writing to the
Romans, he spoke of Jesus Christ as 'descended from David
according to the flesh and **designated Son of God** in power
according to the Spirit of holiness **by his resurrection from the
dead**.'[13]

B. In Mark's Gospel, on the other hand, we find a story of
Jesus at Caesarea Philippi, where he asked his disciples what people
were saying about him and they gave a variety of answers. When
Jesus asked Peter for his opinion he received the reply. '**You are
the Christ**'. The writer of this narrative clearly believed that Jesus
was already the Christ during his ministry and before his death and
resurrection. The narrator further says that Jesus charged his disciples not to mention to anyone that he was the Christ. These references to secrecy in Mark's Gospel are known in modern scholarship
as the Messianic Secret, after the title of a book written in 1901 by
Wilhelm Wrede. He argued that the 'secret' was a primitive literary
invention to reconcile two different traditions about when Jesus
was first acknowledged to be the Messiah — the earlier 'Acts'
account noted in the previous paragraph and the slightly later
'Markan' account that Jesus was already recognized as the Christ
during his ministry.

C. The author of Mark's Gospel, writing at a time (c. 70
C.E.) long after Christians had first accepted Jesus to be the
Messiah, went even further. His story of the baptism of Jesus suggests that that was the event by which he became the Messiah. He
tells us that when Jesus came out of the water he saw the heavens

opened, and the Spirit descended upon him like a dove and a voice came from heaven saying, **"You are my beloved son; with you I am well pleased"**.

This story gave rise in early Christian theology to what was called the 'Adoption theory' of the Person of Christ. In short, Jesus was born as an ordinary human being and remained so until his baptism by John the Baptist, whereupon God adopted him as his Son. This view was eventually declared heretical, though it continued to break out from time to time. It became heretical for the simple reason that the belief that Jesus became the Christ only at his baptism was soon to be surpassed by further changes in the developing tradition.

D. Only in the later Gospels of Matthew and Luke do we find the birth stories of Jesus; these clearly intend to imply that Jesus was the Christ from the time he was born. Whereas Matthew tends to emphasise that Jesus was born to be the future King of the Jews (Messiah or Christ), Luke is more explicit, putting these words into the mouth of the angels; "for to you **is born this day in the city of David a Saviour, who is Christ the Lord**".

A further difference between the birth stories of Luke and Matthew is that Matthew traced the genealogy of Jesus back to Abraham to indicate, as it were, that he was a faithful Jew and a true son of Abraham. But Luke, perhaps because he was a Gentile, traced the genealogy back to Adam to show that Jesus was not only truly representative of humankind also a genuine son of God, for Luke referred to Adam as the son of God.

In tracing this progression backward in time, from post-resurrection days, to the ministry, to his baptism, to his birth, we should note that there is also a shift in emphasis in the terminology being used concerning Jesus. It is a shift from Messiahship to divinity, from the status of Christ to the status of the divine Son of God.

E. This progression backward in time did not stop with the birth of Jesus. When we turn to the Fourth Gospel we find that the process has gone a great deal further. It goes back to the beginning of time. The Fourth Gospel has no place for a birth story, for it dates the Gospel of Jesus Christ from the creation of the world. The one who was to become known as Jesus existed from the beginning but is here referred to as the Logos or Word of God.

> In the beginning was the Word and the Word was with God and **the Word was God** . . . all things were made by him and without him was not anything made that was made . . . and **the Word became flesh** and dwelt among us, full of grace and truth; and we have beheld his glory, glory as of the only Son from the Father . . . grace and truth came through Jesus Christ. No one has ever seen God; the only Son, who is in the bosom of the Father, he has made him known.[14]

Here, the issue of how Jesus became the Christ has been altered to how the Logos (later to be called the only begotten Son of God) became incarnate in human flesh as Jesus. Thus in the course of time the story of how Jesus became God was transformed into the story of how God became human, a process now known as the incarnation.

These selected examples give differing answers to the question of when and how Jesus first became Christ and was eventually acknowledged as divine. When we place them in chronological order of composition (which is what we have just been trying to do), we find clear evidence of a steady progression from A to E. Within the space of about seventy years the chief 'act of God' by which Jesus supposedly became the Christ has moved from after his death, back through his ministry, to his baptism, then to his birth, and finally to the creation itself. What Christian tradition has too often treated as an objective description of Jesus as the Christ turns out to be a succession of subjective judgements illustrating the process by which successive generations came to perceive and worship him as the Christ.

By the end of the first century the memory of the historical Jesus, including his original teaching, had become almost completely hidden behind the Christ of faith as described first by Paul and then by the author of the Fourth Gospel. (I shall refer to him hereafter as John, but we know little about him and most scholars are certain he was not one of Jesus' original disciples.) Neither Paul nor John had ever encountered the historical Jesus face to face. The Jesus of whom Paul speaks is the glorified Christ whom he had met in 'visions and revelations'.[15] John, on his part, paints a portrait of the Christ figure which so towers above the Jesus of the Synoptic Gospels that it almost obliterates him from view.

Whereas the Jesus of the Synoptic Gospels remains a

human figure in spite of his ability to cure the sick and perform miracles, the Jesus presented by John is a divine figure who is in complete command of every situation, even when being tried before Pilate. The Synoptic Jesus speaks in parables and pithy aphorisms and his main topic is the Kingdom of God; he rebukes a person who calls him 'Good Teacher', saying 'Why do you call me good? No one is good but God alone'.[16] The Johannine Christ speaks a great deal about himself and his role, often in long and rambling speeches. He leaves us in no doubt as to his divinity, saying such things as 'He who has seen me has seen the Father . . . I am in the Father and the Father in me'. In particular, he utters a number of I AM sayings, which are especially significant seeing that 'I AM' has strong associations with God because of the Mosaic tradition. Here are some of them: 'I am the bread of life', 'I am the true vine', 'I am the way, the truth and the life'.

Of special interest is this claim of the Johannine Christ: 'I am the resurrection and the life'. As various scholars have stated, the concept of resurrection is dealt with quite differently in the Fourth Gospel. Although John ends his Gospel with resurrection stories in order to follow the pattern of the earlier Gospels, they have really been rendered redundant in this Gospel by the nature of Jesus himself. It is the risen, exalted Jesus who is acting and speaking all through the Gospel: he has become the resurrection.

Within the documents later selected for the New Testament Canon, the Fourth Gospel represents the highest point reached in the progression of thought by which Jesus was becoming God. But the process did not stop there; it continued over the following centuries. As the books that would comprise the Canon became more and more authoritative, the writings of Paul and John were assumed to be firsthand evidence of Jesus as the Christ. Hence they became the raw material used by the long succession of theologians who in debate and controversy teased out the implications of all that had been written. The evolving process by which Jesus became the Christ, as here demonstrated from the New Testament, continued in the post-biblical period.

The year 70 C.E. was a critical point both for Jews and Christians. Not only were the Jews banished from Jerusalem when the city and its Temple were destroyed by the Romans, but the Jewish Christians of Jerusalem were also uprooted and migrated to

Pella across the Jordan river. The rift between Jew and Christian became final; the rift between the Jewish Christians and the rapidly growing Gentile church became steadily wider.

Thus it was that the Gentile Christian movement, as shaped initially by Paul and drawing increasingly on John, became the classical form of Christianity. The thinking of the primitive Jewish church was left behind and eventually forgotten. The Gentile Christians lost their last living contact with the Jewish matrix of their faith and increasingly saw Jesus through Greek eyes. Even Paul, though he gloried in his Jewishness, was very much a Hellenistic Jew.

Unlike the Jews the Gentiles had no expectation of a coming Messiah, so the word Christ (which translates Messiah) simply became a proper name. Jesus the Messiah became Jesus Christ or just Christ. The Gentile mind had no trouble in regarding Jesus as divine. They saw him as the Son of God par excellence — the only Son of God. Indeed the problem soon became not how to proclaim his divinity but how to defend his humanity. The Gnostic wing of the Gentile Christian movement wanted to say that Jesus only 'seemed' or 'appeared' to be a man but was really wholly God all the time. This view, known as Docetism (from *dokeo* meaning 'seem') was eventually condemned by church authorities as heresy, yet it has been present in much popular Christian thought to this day.

As the church struggled to maintain both the full divinity and the full humanity of Jesus it went through a series of theological controversies. It has never been at all clear how Jesus could be 'perfect in Godhead and also perfect in manhood, truly God and truly man' at one and the same time, yet those are the very words authorised by the Council of Chalcedon in 451 C.E. and remain orthodox doctrine to this day.

Various solutions were offered to resolve this apparent contradiction in terms. At first they tried to define just how Jesus was related to God the Creator. The Patripassianists ('suffering Father') so identified Jesus with the Father Creator that it was the latter who suffered and died on the cross. The Modalists (of which there were several varieties) thought of the Father Creator, the Saviour Son, and the life-giving Spirit as being successive modes of the divine monad. The Arians denied the complete divinity of Jesus and saw him as one who had been created by the Father God to be the instrument both of the creation of the world and of the salvation of humankind. Although all these solutions to the apparent contradiction were eventually declared heretical, they nevertheless persisted in popular thought and devotion. Most devout churchgoers today know so little about these ancient controversies that if they were asked to write down their own thoughts about Jesus, many would be surprised to find that, judged by the official doctrines of the church, they are really heretics.

The doctrine of the Holy Trinity attempted to resolve the problem of how Jesus was related to God by declaring him to be the incarnation of the Second Person of the Trinity. Then the church fathers faced the problem of explaining how human nature and divine nature could be united in the one historical personage. The controversy was never universally resolved, for those who disagreed with the findings of the Ecumenical Council of Chalcedon (451 C.E.) were simply excommunicated from the main body. That is how the Nestorians (who affirmed that Jesus had two natures) came to be cut off from the main church; they flourished in Mesopotamia, Persia, and even China, until the spread of Islam, and they still exist today as the Assyrian Christians. At the other extreme were the Monophysites, who asserted that Jesus had only one nature, a divine nature. The Monophysites were also rejected by the main body of the church but continued to exist, largely separate from the rest of Christendom, as the Coptic Church of Egypt and Abyssinia, the Armenian Church, and the Jacobite Syrian Church.

What became Christian Orthodoxy was the following formula arrived at by the Council of Chalcedon. It was intended to steer a middle course between the extremes taken by the Nestorians and the Monophysites. It may be regarded as the final step in the process by which Jesus became God.

> We then, following the Holy fathers, all with one consent, teach men to confess one and the same Son, our Lord Jesus Christ, the same perfect in Godhead and also perfect in manhood; truly God and truly man, of a reasonable soul and body; consubstantial with the Father according to the Godhead, and consubstantial with us according to the Manhood; in all things like unto us, without sin; begotten before all ages of the Father according to the Godhead, and in these latter

days, for us and for our salvation, born of the Virgin Mary, the Mother of God, according to the Manhood; one and the same Christ, Son, Lord, Only-begotten, to be acknowledged in two natures, inconfusedly, unchangeably, indivisibly, inseparably; the distinction of the natures being by no means taken away by the union, but rather the property of each nature being preserved, and concurring in one Person and one Subsistence, not parted nor divided into two persons, but one and the same Son, the only begotten, God the Word, the Lord Jesus Christ; as the prophets from the beginning have declared concerning him, and the Lord Jesus Christ has taught us, and the Creed of the Holy Father has handed down to us.

Today this statement of Christian orthodoxy, couched as it is in Greek concepts which are foreign to us, has become almost nonsensical. The majority of traditional Christians today have probably not even heard of this statement, far less understood it. By the time of the Ecumenical Councils, the Christian understanding of Jesus had moved so far away from the itinerant teacher of Galilee still discernible in the Synoptic Gospels that he was no longer recognizable. One wonders what Jesus himself would have made of all this!

We have traced the stages through which Jesus has progressed in Christian thought: Messiah (Christ), **a** Son of God, the Lord, the Savior, the **only** Son of God, the Logos or Word of God and creator of the world, the incarnation of God, and finally the second person of the Holy Trinity as defined by the Chalcedonian formula. It was only to be expected that this complex structure of doctrine would collapse under its own weight. How that happened and what was to follow is that to which we shall now turn.

Chapter Seven

How did God become man?

he last chapter sketched the rise of what is known in theological circles as Christology; this means the study of the person of Jesus as the Christ. But Christology is only one section of a complete and complex theological system, which also includes such things as Anthropology (doctrine of the human condition), Hamartiology (doctrine of sin), Soteriology (doctrine of salvation), Ecclesiology (doctrine of the church), Eschatology (doctrine of last things).

All these and other doctrines once formed a unified and internally consistent system of thought, which in the eyes of theologians constituted Christian truth. John Dickie (my own theological teacher) even likened this system to a living organism, naming his magnum opus *The Organism of Christian Truth*.[1] But if one section of such a tightly constructed system begins to crumble, the whole system can come tumbling down, and, if likened to an organism, we might say that the failure of one vital organ can bring on its death throes. With the advent of the modern world, this is just what has been happening to 'Christian truth'. During the last five hundred years the complex system of Christian thought has been disintegrating.[2]

It could be said that the first section of the system to decay was ecclesiology. It was this more than anything else which was

87

hotly debated at the Protestant Reformation, and since that time the one, holy, catholic and apostolic church has increasingly lost its unity, its catholicity, its apostolic authority and finally its holiness. It has shown itself in its many extant fragments to be all too human, and in no way much different from the secular world in which it now lives.

Recalling that the church, or community of Christians, was referred to in the New Testament as 'the Body of Christ', we could reasonably expect that the malaise afflicting ecclesiology would very soon affect Christology. The disintegration of Christology took place chiefly in the nineteenth century. That is when the figure of Jesus as the Christ was deconstructed, to use the modern jargon of post-modernism. This took place more or less simultaneously with the deconstruction of the supernatural Christian world of heaven and hell, following on the abolition of Purgatory, which occurred for Protestants at the Reformation. As this supernatural world began to disappear and to be replaced in modern consciousness with the space-time physical universe, we were enabled to understand, not only why Christology was collapsing with it, but also why it developed in the first place in the early centuries.

Christianity burst into life after the death of Jesus amidst the confident expectation of his early return and his restoration of the Kingdom of David. The rediscovery of this eschatological theme in the New Testament was first reported by Reimarus (1694–1768) but it did not become widely accepted until the end of the nineteenth century with the work of Johannes Weiss and Albert Schweitzer. This primitive eschatology permeates the New Testament, being quite explicit in both Paul's writings and the Synoptic Gospels. In apocalyptic thought (such as we have in Revelation) this keenly awaited imminent event was even spoken of as the new heaven and new earth, which would replace the present heaven and earth. Whether Jesus himself actually shared in these eschatological expectations is now open to serious doubt but beginning not long after his death they certainly shaped the thinking of his followers.

By the end of the first century, however, the all too apparent failure of Jesus to return and usher in the expected New World left a vacuum in Christian hopes, one that urgently needed to be filled. It is worth noting that the Fourth Gospel, which comes from that period and which so dramatically portrays Jesus as a divine figure, largely omits the elements of imminent eschatology which pervaded Paul and the Synoptic Gospels. This fact has led some scholars to refer to the 'realised eschatology' of the Fourth Gospel: by this they mean the implication of the Evangelist that Jesus had already returned but had done so in the ongoing life of the church, of which he was king and head. The Fourth Gospel is thus to be seen as a symbolic description of life within the church, under the veil of an account of the ministry of Jesus.

But more than this needed to be done to fill the vacuum left by a failed Second Coming. So Christians of the second and third centuries engaged (unconsciously) in the mental construction of an unseen supernatural world. (This construction, incidentally, somewhat parallels in motivation Aaron's fashioning of the golden calf, when Moses delayed his return from the mountaintop.) The unseen world of Heaven and Hell, (to which Purgatory was later added), replaced the 'new heaven and earth' which had failed to arrive, and it became the primary focus of Christian hope for many centuries to come. Not until this humanly constructed supernatural world began to dissolve into unreality (as it has been doing over the last four hundred years) could there take place the deconstruction of the Christ figure believed to be sitting at the right hand of God's heavenly throne.

The demythologizing of Christ necessarily involved the dissolution of the classical formulations of the Incarnation and of the Holy Trinity. It meant that these two interdependent doctrines must either be abandoned altogether or radically reassessed. Many have understandably opted for the former and consigned them to a place of honour in the museum of outmoded Christian dogmas. Their repudiation, however, re-opened the question of why the pioneers of the Christian path of faith had been so daring in the first place as to declare that 'God was made man'. What led them to incorporate humanity into the concept of God as they did in the doctrine of the Trinity? As we shall now see, the very people most involved in the deconstruction of the doctrines of the Incarnation and Holy Trinity did not simply abandon them; rather they gave them a radically new interpretation, taking them to what could be described as their logical conclusion.

Perhaps the person who more than anyone else pioneered this new interpretation at the beginning of the nineteenth century was the great German philosopher Hegel (1770–1831).[3] At an

early age he became disillusioned with theology, finding the traditional concept of God to be too limited for the greatly expanded
world which humankind had now entered. Like Spinoza before
him, Hegel saw the whole of reality as a unity. God was no longer
to be conceived of as *a person* or even *a being* set over against the
world which he had supposedly created and in which science now
allowed him no place.

Hegel's view of reality has been described as a pantheistic
monism in which the unity of both the physical and the spiritual
world are affirmed as one evolving process. Human self-conscious-
ness is not to be thought of as something apart from God (or
Ultimate Reality) but as its manifestation in a finite form. For the
first time in Western thought, ultimate reality was no longer being
conceived as unchangeable and eternally the same but rather as the
process of divine self-realization. The One who had traditionally
been conceived as the Author of change had now become identified with the process of change itself. Hegel was suggesting these
things fifty years before Darwin's theory of evolution began to grip
the European mind and 150 years before Teilhard de Chardin gave
biological evolution a more cosmic and spiritual interpretation.

Within this new vision of reality Hegel proceeded to offer
some daring new interpretations of the leading Christian themes.
At a time when most people were still treating the story of Adam
and Eve as historical, Hegel took it to be a myth or parable in
which he found a deep philosophical meaning. Paradise represented
the life of animal-like innocence in which there was as yet no awareness of good and evil; it was a state prior to the emergence of the
human condition. Hegel interpreted the story of Adam and Eve
not as 'the Fall' of humankind but as 'the Rise'; humankind had
their eyes opened, became aware of good and evil, and were hence
given both the freedom to become decision-making creatures and
the attendant responsibility.

Similarly Hegel gave a radically new interpretation to the
Incarnation. For him the idea of Christ as both divine and human
affirmed at once the humanity of God and the divinity of
humankind. It symbolized the fact that the gulf between God and
humankind was being obliterated and that God and humans were
becoming one (Christians had long called it reconciliation). Hegel
agreed with Christian orthodoxy that the death of Christ was the

key to it all, for it symbolically represented the death of God as 'a being'. 'God is dead', said Hegel, noting that he found this phrase in a Lutheran hymn. What had died on the cross, symbolized in divine/human Jesus, was the existence of God as an individual being, standing over against us human beings.

What followed the death of God on the cross, of course, was the resurrection. Again we find that Hegel was among the first of modern thinkers to treat the resurrection narratives of Jesus as symbolic. The God who came to life again in the resurrection of Christ was the Spirit which came upon the friends of Jesus, enabling them to see and experience the true significance of the Incarnation. In other words, the Christ figure symbolized the fact that God had become one with humankind — God was made man!

These are a few of the seed thoughts coming from Hegel two centuries ago. No wonder Paul Tillich said, 'Hegel is in some sense the centre and the turning-point . . . of a world-historical movement which has directly or indirectly influenced our whole century'.[4] This is because he captured the imagination of those who, like himself, either sensed or were convinced that the world had entered a new, post-theistic age. Humankind needed a new vision, a new understanding of the nature of reality.

But after giving utterance to these theological insights in his earlier years, Hegel later devoted himself wholly to philosophy. It was left to his left-wing disciples ('young Hegelians', as they were called) to nurture to maturity the seed-thoughts we have briefly glimpsed. They moved to even more radical positions, sometimes strongly critical of the residue of traditional Christian thought still present in Hegel. Strauss drove a wedge between the mythical and historical elements in the Christian tradition and Feuerbach turned Hegel's system upside down, showing that spirit had evolved out of things material, rather than the other way round.

First came David Strauss[5] (1808–1874). Since 1843, when he wrote his epoch-making book *The Life of Jesus Critically Examined*, it has been necessary in biblical scholarship to distinguish between what he later called 'The Jesus of History' and 'The Christ of Faith'. The term 'Jesus of History' (or 'the historical Jesus') refers to the actual person who lived and taught in ancient Galilee. The life of this Jesus is open to historical investigation.

The term 'Christ of Faith' refers to the figure worshipped by Christians as divine, the Son of God, and Saviour of the world. This figure is not open to historical enquiry for he 'lives' in the hearts and minds of those who worship him.

Prompted by the work of Strauss, biblical scholars took up the task of recovering a reliable picture of the historical Jesus. This proved exceedingly difficult to achieve, because the portrait was largely hidden behind the many faces of Christ created by devout imagination during the first century and later. By the beginning of the twentieth century Albert Schweitzer, surveying all the modern 'lives of Jesus' in his *The Quest of the Historical Jesus* (1906) concluded they were faulty. He claimed that this elusive Jesus had 'returned to his own time' and cannot be extracted from it; we must be content with the 'mighty spiritual force which streamed from him'.

Yet, in the latter part of the twentieth century a community of scholars known as the Jesus Seminar[6] resumed the quest for the historical Jesus and claims to have uncovered at least his footprints and voiceprints. What their efforts show is that the historical Jesus was truly human in every way, even to being a man of his own times.

The historical Jesus was not separated from his fellow-humans by a great gulf as the glorified Christ was. Jesus was wholly human. This is at least one of the various meanings which can be offered for the term 'son of man', so frequently found in the Gospels in reference to Jesus. In the Hebrew Bible 'son of Adam' (humankind) simply meant 'human being' and was a way of emphasizing the human condition. In the book of Ezekiel it was frequently placed in the mouth of God in addressing the prophet. It was used similarly in Job 25:6 and Psalm 8:4. Only in later Christian apocalyptic thought did it assume a more esoteric connotation as the Christian community tried to extract a messianic meaning out of a different but somewhat parallel Aramaic term found in Daniel 7:13.

The term 'son of man', therefore, pointed primarily to someone's humanity and is not unlike the term adopted by the modern Jewish philosopher and writer, Asher Ginzberg (1856-1927), who founded 'cultural Zionism'. He preferred to call himself Ahad Ha-am, which means 'one of the people'. Jesus, in his day, was 'one of the people', in contrast with the Pharisees who were the overtly 'religious' people of the day. Jesus mixed with prostitutes, lepers, and tax-gatherers. He identified with 'the common people' and joined in their feasting, as his enemies loved to point out. Jesus did not choose the ascetic lifestyle of John the Baptist, but enjoyed life to the full. In spite of this, or perhaps because of it, Jesus was seen by his followers as one who had brought heavenly values down to earth. His teaching and the manner of his life enabled people to sense the presence of the divine in the affairs of ordinary daily life.

The recovery of the full humanity of Jesus led Strauss to interpret the doctrine of the Incarnation in a new and more extensive way. Following Hegel, he said the incarnation portrays in a symbolic fashion the spiritual process of the cosmos. It means at one and the same time the humanization of God and the divinization of humankind. The traditional interpretation restricted the Incarnation to one human person, namely the man Jesus of Nazareth, but this was now being extended to the whole of humankind.

The idea that God could become enfleshed even in one special person was more than most first century Jews could accept. To this day Jews and Muslims, being pure theists, reject the very possibility of incarnation. Even Christianity in the long run largely lost sight of its real significance, in spite of its being explicitly spelt out in the creeds. First, as we have seen, there was a strong tendency for the humanity of Jesus to be replaced by the docetic appearance of a heavenly figure. The historical Jesus became treated as an avatar of God in the much the same way as, in Hindu tradition, Krishna was worshipped as an avatar of the god Vishnu. Second, the devotional image of the glorified Christ sitting in heavenly glory was a far cry from the simple teacher of Galilee. The humanity of Jesus had been shed like the dead shell of the chrysalis from which the butterfly has emerged. In Christian thought and practice, even if not in the liturgy, the incarnation was being denied. The denial of the incarnation in turn affected the validity of the doctrine of the trinity, and this is the reason why Christianity showed a strong tendency to revert to theism. Orthodox Christianity, in its modern defence of theism, has failed to appreciate the significance of its own most central doctrines.

If it was impossible for Jews and Muslims to accept that God had become enfleshed in one special person (and difficult even for Christians adequately to retain it), the idea that God could become enfleshed in humanity as a whole was almost from the beginning more than even Christians were able to accept. Yet the seeds of this wider interpretation of the incarnation were already present in the New Testament, but these seeds were prevented from germinating in much the same way and for much the same reasons as the new status and roles afforded to women in the first century were not allowed to flourish and were lost from sight.

Paul, we must remember, spoke of Christ as the embodiment of the whole human race. Just as he regarded the first Adam as embodying the whole human race, so he spoke of the Christ as the New Adam, i.e. the embodiment of the new humankind. That is why Paul spoke of all Christians as being 'in Christ'. He spoke of Christians as being new creatures or new beings. He conceived of them as participating in the continuing incarnation.

Gordon Kaufman has given his support to this wider interpretation view of the incarnation. He pointed out that 'Christ' is used in the New Testament not exclusively as a reference to Jesus but to a range of events surrounding and including Jesus; and these include the whole new order of relationships of humans to God and to one another within the early Christian community. He said that to tie the incarnation to a single individual (as classical Christianity eventually did) renders it not only paradoxical but also almost unintelligible.[7]

Thus, from the beginning, and continuing in later intimations, the New Testament has incorporated the seed-thought that humanity itself was to be the enfleshment or incarnation of the divine. This is reflected in the way the Eastern Orthodox Church speaks of the Christian life as the process of 'deification'. Even Aquinas said that the Incarnation is the exaltation of human nature and consummation of the universe.

The first modern theologian to expound this new way of understanding the Incarnation was another young Hegelian, Ludwig Feuerbach. He followed hard on the heels of David Strauss with his book, *The Essence of Christianity*. There he contrasted the False or Theological Meaning of the Incarnation with the True or Humanistic Meaning of the Incarnation. In Christian orthodoxy, as we have seen, the humanity of Jesus had been taken up into glory and lost sight of within the heavenly Trinity. For Feuerbach the Incarnation meant quite the reverse of that. It said that 'God became man', meaning that the divine had come down to earth, to reside permanently within humanity.

For Feuerbach the deconstruction of the Christ figure (as achieved by Strauss) enabled the long hidden truth of the doctrine of the incarnation to come to light. It thus spelt the end of theism, (as Hegel had said) for it declared that the God who was mythically conceived to be sitting upon a heavenly throne had come down to dwell in human flesh — in all human flesh. This is why the Incarnation, properly understood, marked such a turning point in human history.

Following the example of the New Testament declaration that 'God is love', Feuerbach took the being of God to be nothing else but the highest moral values, such as love, justice, and compassion, and these, henceforth, were to be manifested within the human race. This means, first, that we humans must live without the divine heavenly props thought to exist in the past. 'We must be mature as God is mature',[8] as Jesus himself is quoted in the Sermon on the Mount. Second, the Incarnation signifies that we must now play on the earth the role which theism always assigned to an objective, supernatural god. Not only is the heavenly throne empty but heaven itself is an empty void.

Feuerbach's argument is a fascinating tour de force. He appeals to the most basic Christian doctrine — that of the Incarnation — to achieve the deconstruction of the Christian system of belief, which revolves round God and Christ. In the last chapter we traced the steps by which Jesus became the Christ - in other words, how the human condition became elevated to the divine. By the end of the first century this was, ironically, being described in the Fourth Gospel by words which proclaimed the exact opposite: 'the Word (being God) had become human flesh'. The process had come full circle. The real essence of Christianity, said Feuerbach, is not that Jesus became God but that God became human. The life and death of Jesus truly marked a turning point in human history!

But if this is so, why has it taken us so long to see it this way? Was it really necessary, symbolically speaking, for Jesus to be taken up into glory and deified so that in our recovery of his humanity he could bring the divine down into us? Feuerbach was so far ahead of his time that he was completely rejected and his insights lost sight of for more than a century. Although Nietzsche had little regard for Feuerbach, he nevertheless echoed his interpretation of the Incarnation, saying, 'That God became man shows only that man is not to seek his bliss in eternity but to found his heaven on earth; the delusion of a supraterrestrial world has placed the spirit of man in a false relation to the terrestrial: it was the product of the People's childhood'.[9]

The reason it took so long for the full significance of the Incarnation to be fully appreciated is that it had to wait until the whole supernatural world constructed in the early centuries had collapsed. This occurred at the second Axial Period when, out of the disintegrating church structure, there emerged the modern secular world. At last we are in a position to appreciate the full import of the Incarnation: the modern secular world can now be seen as the logical development of the doctrine of the incarnation and the legitimate continuation of the Judeo-Christian path of faith.

Such a view is an anathema to orthodox Christians. There has been great reluctance on the part of the Christian churches to see any connection at all between Christianity and the modern secular world. They customarily regard the latter as something foreign and to be held at bay. In more extreme circles the secular world is treated as the work of the devil and an enemy to be fought.

By contrast, the relationship between the secular world and Christian doctrine of the incarnation is now being taken more seriously in theological circles. In 1889 Charles Gore edited a symposium of Essays on 'The Religion of the Incarnation' called *Lux Mundi*. They were written, he said, out of the conviction that the epoch from which they sprang was 'one of profound transformation, intellectual and social, abounding in new needs, new points of view, new questions',[10] an epoch which signalled that 'theology must take a new development'.

One of the contributors, J. R. Illingworth, regarded secular thought not as the enemy of Christianity but as that which 'often corrected and counteracted the evil of a Christianity grown professional and false and foul'. 'Secular civilization has co-operated with Christianity to produce the modern world. It is nothing less than the providential correlative and counterpart of the incarnation'.[11]

By the middle of the twentieth century, William Temple, the scholarly archbishop of Canterbury, declared that Christianity was 'the most materialist of all the great religions'.[12] Similarly, while reflecting in his prison cell, Dietrich Bonhoeffer, the German theologian imprisoned by Hitler, concluded that people could no longer be religious in the traditional way; this led him to explore the outlines of what was later called 'secular Christianity'. The Scottish theologian Ronald Gregor Smith confessed he found it very difficult to assign any meaning to the word God and questioned whether a theistic worldview was any longer essential for Christianity; he said he had come to regard Christ as 'the truly secular man'.

In the 1960s a group of radical theologians solemnly announced 'the Death of God'; it was 150 years after Hegel and eighty years after Nietzsche! One of these was Thomas Altizer, who in his *The Gospel of Christian Atheism,* claimed that the Christian doctrine of the Incarnation already acknowledged that 'God' had emptied himself out in Christ. When Christ died, God also died. But as Christ rose again, so God rose again; but he did so in human history. As Altizer later expressed it, 'God has actually become incarnate in the world, embodying himself at the centre of history and life'.[8]

I now haul my two kites back to earth. I have tried to show in the first place that Christianity made a radical departure from pure theism in the early centuries by means of its key doctrines of the Incarnation and the Holy Trinity. Although there has been a strong tendency for Christianity to revert to theism, particularly in modern times as the system of Christian doctrine has been disintegrating, Christianity already began in ancient times to walk a path of faith which would eventually dispense with the theistic God. Since the Second Axial Period, the broad stream of Western and Christian-based culture has been now learning how to walk even further along that non-theistic path.

In the second place, it is an indisputable fact of history that the modern secular world emerged out of the matrix of a Western culture long nurtured and shaped by Christianity. It was in the

Christian West that the Second Axial Period originated, with its widespread questioning of past authorities and its fresh emphasis on this-worldliness and on all human enterprise. This suggests that there is some intrinsic relationship between the Christian West and the modern secular world, even though, as in many historical developments, this is difficult to establish with any certainty. The connection may be traced, among other factors, to the central Christian doctrine of the Incarnation — the declaration that 'God had been made man'. The modern secular world is not merely the accidental consequence of the Christian West but the logical development of its most basic doctrine.

It can, of course, be argued that Christianity without the theistic God is no longer Christianity but humanism. For this reason the word 'humanism' is strongly disliked in conservative Christian circles. We need here to clarify its meaning. As the term humanism is used today, it usually does imply non-theism, but it did not do so when it was first used. The term originated during the Renaissance and basically refers to all philosophies and sets of attitudes which acknowledge positive value in the human condition and which concede to humankind the right to be free, to think for itself, and to be responsible for its own destiny.

One of the best descriptions of humanism is that of Pico della Mirandola (1463–1494) in his *Oration on the Dignity of Man*. There he tells us that the reason why God made man at the close of creation was in order that we might come to know the laws of the universe, to love its beauty, and to admire its greatness. He suggested that God told Adam that he had created him to be neither heavenly nor earthly but to be free to shape himself into whatever form he chose and to bear responsibility for the consequences of his decisions. Along with other Renaissance humanists including the great scholar Erasmus, Mirandola did not question the reality of God. Rather, they wished to reaffirm the positive values and potential of the human condition. This was something which had been taken away by traditional Christianity with its emphasis on the consequences of the Fall and its dogmas of original sin and of absolute dependence on divine grace.

The doctrine of the Incarnation gives strong support to such a view of the human condition, though to what extent the humanists were consciously aware of it we do not know. The assertion that God had become man (particularly when given the wider interpretation discussed above) focused attention on the potential inherent in the human condition — and suggested that humankind was capable of embodying all the values usually attributed to God. Strangely enough, the way Christian devotion focused on the womb of Mary gave emphasis to this very point, even though it used mythical language to do so. Indeed the whole cult of the Virgin Mary can be construed as a symbolic picture of how Mother Church has provided the womb from which has been born the new secular mankind, which is in the process of being divinized.

So though the Renaissance humanists were not non-theists, they did switch attention away from heaven and back to earth. They did refocus attention on the human condition. They did prepare the soil for the humanist seeds in the original doctrine of the Incarnation to germinate. And from where did those seeds come? That is what we shall now explore. It is all too little appreciated that from the beginning humanism has been a hidden current in the Judeo-Christian cultural stream. To this we now turn.

Chapter Eight

Where did Christian humanism begin?

ver forty years ago, while travelling in a Brisbane suburban train, I found myself sitting beside a person who volunteered to me he was a Baptist minister. When I told him, in answer to his question, that I taught Old Testament Studies at a theological college, he said to me, 'There are three books of the Old Testament for which I have no respect at all'. So I asked him to name them and tell me why he had such a low opinion of them, even though they were in Holy Scripture. He replied, 'The Book of Esther never mentions "God" at all, the Song of Songs is a collection of erotic love-songs, and Ecclesiastes was written by an agnostic'. This clergyman was clearly no fundamentalist, being so critical of some books in the Bible, but he expressed what has long been a fairly common attitude to some books in the Bible.

Christians have long felt uncomfortable with some books of the Bible. They dealt with the erotic character of the Song of Songs by allegorizing it into a symbolic account of the love of Christ for his church, but some books they simply ignored. Theologians, even more than preachers, gave scant attention to what did not suit their purposes, often confining their attention very narrowly to the Pauline Epistles, particularly Romans and Galatians. Luther disparagingly described the letter of James as an

epistle of straw and said he would laugh at it as a lie if it were not
in the Bible. He disliked the way it urged Christians to show their
faith by their works. The neglected books we are about to discuss
have much affinity with James. They became the forgotten section
of Holy Scripture because they were found to be somewhat earthy,
much more secular than the rest, and all too human.

Christians had a bible from the beginning, having inherited all the Holy Books of the Jews. These became known as the
Old Testament only after the New Testament was added in the
third century. Nearly all the material in the Old Testament had its
origin in oral tradition, since this was the medium through which
all pre-literate societies transmitted their cultural knowledge.
Within Israel's oral tradition there developed at least four different
streams of interest, and these continued to be clearly distinguish-
able even after they had been committed to writing.

First there is the founding tradition of the people of Israel;
it narrates the Hebrew Exodus from Egypt and the giving of the
Law on Mt Sinai. It is sometimes known as the five books of
Moses, because of the later belief that he wrote it. The Jews call it
the Torah or Law (though it contains much more than what we
usually associate with the term 'law'). It began with an introduc-
tion (now known as Genesis) which contains legendary stories
stretching from the Creation to the patriarchs, ending with the
story of Joseph. The Torah was put into its final form by priestly
scribes about 400 B.C.E. and was the first section of Jewish
Scriptures to be regarded as sacred; its pre-eminence remains clear
in synagogue practice to this day.

The second stream of Jewish interest was the Prophetic.
This is found chiefly in the books of the Prophets, which were put
together in some cases by the prophets themselves but more often
by those impressed by what the prophets had said and done. The
prophets were believed to be in receipt of oracular messages direct
from God, although what they said often brought them into sharp
conflict with the priests. While both groups remained loyal to the
basic outlines of the Mosaic Tradition, the concern of the priests
was meticulously to preserve it unchanged, whereas the prophets
were God's spokespersons about current affairs events soon to
come. The priests had their eyes on the past; the prophets were
looking to the future.

A third stream of interest was the tradition of the Kingdom. This was concerned with the rise of the monarchy and the divine authorization of the Davidic dynasty, which came to be regarded as equally essential to Israel's existence as the Torah. This stream found literary expression chiefly in Samuel, Kings, and Chronicles, but is reflected elsewhere, as in some psalms. Those responsible for committing this stream to writing were the chroniclers, state officials, and other royalists. The books of Joshua, Judges, Samuel, and Kings came to be known as the Former Prophets, perhaps because the early prophets played a leading role in the establishment of the Kingdom.

There was yet a fourth stream of interest, often referred to now as the Wisdom Literature. This is neither priestly, nor prophetic, nor royalist. It seems to have arisen initially out of the folklore of ordinary people, as they reflected on the daily round of living and the social problems arising from personal relationships. It showed little interest in the official religious practices and can legitimately be termed secular (meaning 'this-worldly') in its concerns. The people responsible for collecting and preserving these many observations on life are commonly referred to by today's scholars as the sages, for as time went on they not only collected anonymous sayings but also began to compose longer tractates in the same vein. In Jeremiah 18:18 we find that priest, sage and prophet are accorded equal status. It has even been suggested that the sages established schools in which the Wisdom writings were taught and discussed.

The Jews themselves did not regard their holy writings to be all of equal standing but divided them into sections known as 'The Law, the Prophets, and the Writings. The Law (or Torah) was treated as Holy Scripture first class, the Prophets were deemed next in importance, while bringing up the rear were the Writings. This third section was still being added to when Christianity inherited the Jewish Scriptures. This is why the Greek version (used by the Gentile church and known today as the Septuagint), is included among the Writings books, which are now labelled the Apocrypha. The Protestant Reformers rejected these as Holy Scripture because they were not found in the Hebrew Bible.

What this fact demonstrates is that the Wisdom stream of Jewish thought was thriving and indeed growing at the time of

Christian origins, even though the Jews did not value it as highly as they did the Torah or the Prophets, which were then regarded as complete. The Wisdom books which gained a place in the Christian Bible are Proverbs, Job, Ecclesiastes, some Psalms, Ecclesiasticus (also known as The Wisdom of Jesus ben Sirach), and the Wisdom of Solomon. There is reason to believe that these represent only a small selection of what Israel's sages either collected or personally produced.[1]

With one exception these books were composed in Hebrew; only the Wisdom of Solomon seems to have originated in Greek. Even so, it imitated the poetical structure of the others, a kind of versification which is technically known today as parallelism. This took the form of couplets in which the second half of the verse confirmed the first half, either by extending its meaning or by repeating it in one of a variety of ways. For example, 'A wise son makes a glad father, but a foolish son is a sorrow to his mother'.[2] Versification not only gave to Wisdom an appropriate dignity but it made it much easier to commit to memory in order to make it part of one's readily available store of guiding principles.

The earliest expression of Wisdom came in the form of short pithy aphorisms or maxims of the kind just quoted. They were similar to proverbial sayings found in every culture, such as our 'Beggars can't be choosers', and 'A stitch in time saves nine'. Many of these are found embedded in Proverbs and Ecclesiasticus. They offer observations about natural phenomena and frequently occurring human situations; they prescribe the patterns of behaviour to follow if one wishes to live a social life which is harmonious, satisfying, and free of conflict.

But often in Proverbs, even more in Ecclesiasticus, and throughout the Wisdom of Solomon we find not just isolated maxims but collections of couplets on a common theme. This shows that the sages were much more than collectors of popular folklore. They were also creative, moving on from anonymous proverbs to the composition of sustained reflections on various aspects of life. They explored and expounded what came to be called Wisdom.

The Hebrew word for wisdom, *hokhma*, is frequently associated with words meaning 'understanding' and 'knowledge'. It can refer to a wide variety of things, such as political insight, knowledge of nature, discernment of right and wrong, and even techni-

cal skill. The concerns of wisdom were quite pragmatic and sometimes even sounded mundane. The sages (at least originally) did
not attempt to wrestle with ultimate questions. They believed that
the world should be accepted just as it is and that one should discover and follow the rules of the game rather than attempt to
change the rules to suit oneself.

Wisdom was most commonly expressed in a form called a
mashal, a term covering anything from one-liners to parabolic narratives. The root meaning of this word is 'to be like', and although
mashal has been usually rendered as 'proverb', it can just as readily
be translated as 'parable'. Wisdom was thus frequently expressed in
the form of comparisons (or mini-parables) as in:

> He who meddles in a quarrel not his own
> is like one who takes a passing dog by the ears.
> Like a madman who throws firebrands, arrows and death,
> is the man who deceives his neighbour and says, 'I am only
> joking!'[3]

Indeed, the Greek Old Testament (or Septuagint) nearly
always translated *mashal* with the Greek term *parabole*, the very
word used in the New Testament with reference to the parables of
Jesus.

These sustained compositions of couplets eventually led to
long and more integrated works such as Job and Ecclesiastes. Job
takes the form of a carefully constructed drama on the issue of why
the innocent often suffer while the wicked go unpunished.
(Tennyson even judged Job to be the greatest poem of all time!)
Ecclesiastes, on the other hand, is a monologue, or personal confession, of a man wrestling with the ultimate issues of life and finding no answers.

When we compare the Wisdom books with the other three
streams of interest in the Old Testament, the first thing that strikes
us is the almost complete absence of the great themes which dom-
inate elsewhere — the destiny of Israel as a people, the Covenant
relationship between Yahweh and Israel, the Exodus Tradition, the
Davidic dynasty, and the prophetic expectation of divine intervention in the flow of history. It's not that the sages did not know
about these themes of Israel's faith, for they do occasionally mention God or Yahweh; it's rather that these subjects have become all

but irrelevant to daily life and therefore relegated to the margins of their field of interest.

In short, the sages were not concerned with the destiny of the Israelite people, as were the other three streams. They focused on all humankind, eventually (as in Ecclesiastes) exploring even the issue of what it means to be human. That is why the sages felt free to borrow from their counterparts in other cultures, especially Egyptian and Mesopotamian. As von Rad observed, 'To a greater extent than is the case in any other intellectual or religious sphere, Israel's Wisdom has borrowed from neighboring cultures'[4]. There is no doubt that Proverbs 22:17–23:14 depends on a composition of the Egyptian Amen-en-opet, for the similarities are too close to be co-incidental. There is also some similarity with the Aramaic Proverbs of Ahikar. The Wisdom stream was thus very cosmopolitan; today we would say it was 'global' in its outreach.

Perhaps this is why the sages came to associate wisdom with Solomon. He may well have been a patron of the arts but why should he come to be so identified with wisdom? It can hardly have been for his political prowess, for some of his policies showed a singular lack of wisdom. He ruled like an Eastern potentate; to support his extravagant life style he subjected his people to such severe taxation and forced labour that on his death the greater part of his kingdom revolted and rejected the Davidic dynasty for ever.

Yet the Book of Proverbs was traditionally ascribed to him; the Wisdom of Solomon bears his name; the writer of Ecclesiastes deliberately published his work in the name of Solomon; the Song of Songs (perhaps more appropriately, in view of its sexually suggestive language!) was said to have been written by him.

What impressed the Wisdom schools about the reign of Solomon was that along with trade and other international relationships it developed a free interchange of cultural resources. It became famous not only for its material prosperity and lavish building programmes, but also for its cultural creativity. The fame of Solomon's kingdom is said to have become the talk of the then known world. The Queen of Sheba made her celebrated visit to inspect for herself the wealth and power of the famous king and to discover the secret of his wisdom. Many scholars have concluded that the first attempts to write an epic history for Israel were also undertaken during the Solomonic period. In view of all this, it is not so surprising that the sages associated the reign of Solomon with the flowering of wisdom.

Jesus ben Sirach (writing much later) saw Solomon as the wise man par excellence. In his mini-epic poem on the heroes of Israelite tradition, which starts with 'Let us now praise famous men . . . ' he wrote of Solomon:

> How wise you became in your youth!
> You overflowed like a river with understanding.
> Your soul covered the earth,
> and you filled it with parables and riddles.
> Your name reached to far-off lands,
> and you were loved for your peace.
> For your songs and proverbs and parables,
> and for your interpretations, the countries marvelled at you.[5]

His reference here was the story in the Kingdom tradition, which tells that early in his reign Solomon had a dream in which he asked God for an understanding mind to enable him to govern his people. In his dream he was assured by God that because he had asked for this rather than for riches or victory over his enemies, he would not only be given a wise and discerning mind, but he would receive riches and honour as a divine bonus.[6]

On waking from his dream, Solomon's ability to demonstrate wisdom was almost immediately tested. In those days the King was expected to act as the final court of appeal in dispensing justice to his subjects. So there came to him two prostitutes who lived in the same house and who had both recently given birth to offspring. But one infant had died in the night and both mothers were now laying claim to the living child. Solomon was challenged to decide which one was the true mother. He called for a sword to divide the living child in two so that each woman might receive her just half. Immediately, the real mother called out for the child to be given to the other so that its life would be spared. Solomon then delivered the child to that woman, for, by showing genuine love for the infant, she was clearly the true mother. The story suggests that by this appeal to human psychology Solomon showed his wisdom, and his fame spread throughout the world.

To be sure, Solomon did make some wise governmental decisions. He was not a man of blood and conflict as his father David had been, for he had not had to fight his way to the top.

Solomon may have been born with a silver spoon in his mouth, but he had taken full advantage of his opportunities; thus in the eyes of the sages he had shown wisdom. He dealt firmly and efficiently with the family disunity which had come to the fore in his father's declining years. He opened up healthy diplomatic relationships with surrounding nations, and these he cemented according to the accepted practice of the day by taking foreign wives into the royal harem. Then he provided the kingdom with an efficient economy, by developing new industries. He has been called the 'copper king' because of the mining he promoted near the Gulf of Aqabah. He engaged in a lucrative horse and chariot trade. As the sages judged it, the splendour and wealth of the Solomonic kingdom were not due to any divine intervention nor did they result from military conquest; they were due to Solomon's wisdom.

The Wisdom tradition valued peace and believed all strife and conflict could be avoided if only wisdom were allowed to prevail. The sages encouraged personal effort and individual initiative. They believed humans should not look outside of themselves, expecting others to provide for them; rather, humans had it within them to achieve prosperity and peace and to make a success of life. It was a matter of distinguishing clearly between right and wrong modes of behaviour, of avoiding everything which is evil, and of choosing that which is right and good.

Above all people must be diligent and industrious. The sages were scathing about those who were slothful:

> Go to the ant, O sluggard: Consider her ways and be wise.
> Without having any chief, officer or ruler,
> She prepares her food in summer, and gathers her sustenance in harvest.
> How long will you lie there, O sluggard? When will you arise from your sleep?
> A little sleep, a little slumber, a little folding of the hands to rest;
> And poverty will come upon you like a vagabond,
> And want like an armed man.[7]

In the Wisdom literature the focus of attention was not, as in the Mosaic Tradition, on God, the sacrifices, and the Temple; it was on how humans live their daily life and how to deal with its problems and frustrations. They did occasionally refer to 'God' or 'the Lord', and even identified reverence for God as the beginning of Wisdom; but they introduced the divine names as if they were simply part of the universally accepted cultural vocabulary. It was as if the term 'God' had become for them a symbol for the cosmic order of the natural world and it was this which had to be respected and even reverenced. Sometimes God was almost a synonym for Fate, in the sense of 'what will be will be!' For example, Jesus ben Sirach said, 'Good things and bad, life and death, poverty and wealth come from the Lord'.[8] 'God' symbolized all that humans must learn to accept about the way the world is.

There is an interesting parallel between the way the Hebrew sages refer to God and the way Confucius refers to Heaven. For example, Confucius comments, 'There are three things of which Man at his best stands in awe: the commands of Heaven, important people, the words of the sages'. Indeed, there is a strange affinity between the Hebrew Wisdom tradition and the Analects of Confucius. Because these came out of two such entirely different cultures, all that they had in common was their humanity. The fact that we find such parallels as these only goes to emphasize the humanism of Hebrew wisdom.

Where the prophets or the psalmists might have spoken about the attributes of God, the sages preferred to talked about Wisdom, speaking as if it were a personal entity and a feminine one at that! The many different metaphors the sages applied to Wisdom imply that they were aware they were using poetic imagery. To use modern terminology, they were consciously objectifying the quality of wisdom, discernible in human behaviour. They spoke of Wisdom in much the same way as the Greeks later spoke of the Logos (Reason); Wisdom had existed from the beginning of time, just as the Logos had. Like the Logos, Wisdom emanated **from** God and **was** God: indeed God both begot and collaborated with Wisdom in the process of creating the world.[9] In the Wisdom of Solomon we read:

> For wisdom is more mobile than any motion:
> Because of her pureness she pervades and penetrates all things.
> For she is a breath of the power of God,
> And a pure emanation of the glory of the Almighty;
> Therefore nothing defiled gains entrance into her.
> For she is a reflection of eternal light,

A spotless mirror of the working of God,
And an image of his goodness.[10]

The time would eventually come (as it has in modern times) when it would be realised that what the sages were consciously doing with the concept of Wisdom could also explain the rise of the concept of God. It was far too early in cultural evolution for us to expect the sages to see the connection, for they lived in a time when only a fool would say, 'There is no God'.[11] Nevertheless the sages had already relegated God-talk to the periphery of their concerns. They did not expect to hear any direct message from God, as the prophets did, nor did they appeal to God to solve their problems for them.

So the sages showed little interest in what we might call the conventional religious beliefs and practices of their day. This does not mean they were irreligious but rather that, for them, religion had more to do with the way people lived their daily lives; the mediaeval division of activities into religious and secular must not be applied to the ancient world. That is why the prophets could speak so much about social justice and the will of Yahweh for the market-place. Religion for the sages was much like that which James defined in these words: 'Religion that is pure and undefiled before God is this: to visit orphans and widows in their affliction, and to keep oneself unstained from the world'.[12]

The sages believed people had to take full responsibility for their lives and to solve their own problems, first by making a proper study of life in the world, by learning what it could tell them, and, finally, by showing the necessary courage and determination to make the right responses. This was the way of Wisdom. Wise people were those who strove to find their proper role in whatever situation they found themselves. Since most things in life could not be changed, they had to learn how to make the most of the choices which still lay open.

Whereas the Torah, the Prophets, and the Kingdom tradition were concerned with the destiny of Israel as a people, the Wisdom stream was concerned with the life of the individual person. The commandments of the Torah were addressed to Israel as a people rather than to the Israelite. And, as the prophets kept reminding Israel, if the people of Israel failed to honour its covenant with Yahweh, it was the whole body of Israel which would suffer. There is much to be said in favour of acknowledging community responsibility, as we know even to this day, but it also has the negative effect of diminishing individual identity and personal initiative, to say nothing of discouraging a person from taking full responsibility for his/her own destiny.

These aspects of individualism were the great strengths of the Wisdom stream and even the prophets eventually had to take them on board. This they did when Jeremiah and Ezekiel declared that, if a person committed a mortal sin, he alone should die for it; no person should be held responsible for the sins of another.[13] They held up to criticism an ancient proverb which was being continually quoted in the land of Israel to explain undeserved suffering of innocent individuals: 'The fathers have eaten sour grapes, and the children's teeth are set on edge'.[14] It is interesting that we do not find this proverb quoted in the Wisdom literature. Perhaps the sages had already rejected it; after all, most of what they said was in sharp conflict with it.

But if the prophets had to modify their message at the time of the Babylonian Exile, so also did the sages. They had long tried to explain away the undeserved suffering of the righteous in a way different from the above proverb. They said, 'If the righteous is requited on earth, how much more the wicked and the sinner!'[15] One simply had to be patient and wait long enough to find that, in the end, the righteous would prosper while the way of the wicked would lead to disaster. It was against this dogma of the earlier sages that the author of Job mounted his dramatic challenge. The traditional answer of the sages was expressed in a variety of ways through the mouths of the 'comforters'. But Job was having none of it. In the end he challenged God to defend his own actions; the comforters regarded this as blasphemy and self-righteous human hubris, so they left him in disgust.

At last Yahweh answered Job out of the whirlwind with a long list of rhetorical questions which were intended to shame Job into acknowledging that in his ignorance he did not really know what he was talking about. This is the final put-down in any argument and it leaves nothing more to be said. So theists like to interpret the book of Job as the vindication of theism, in that God must always have the last word and humans are in no position to challenge him. But this is to forget that even the speeches put into the mouth of Yahweh were composed by humans! It is analogous to the fact that as soon as we acknowledge the human authorship of the books of the Bible, we initiate the collapse of the fundamentalist's claim that everything written in the Bible is true.

Thus, the author of the book of Job, having raised a very serious moral problem about theism, actually left it unresolved. It was destined to surface many times again and not least during and after the Second Axial Period. The philosopher Leibniz (1646–1716) coined a special term for it — theodicy. It is the problem of how to reconcile the belief in an almighty and all-loving God with the phenomenon of massive evils descending upon humankind. Already in the eighteenth century the Lisbon earthquake of 1755 made it increasingly difficult for European theists to defend God's apparent indifference to innocent suffering. The Nazi holocaust of the Jewish people finally convinced many theologians, Jewish and Christian, that the personal God of theism is dead. 'Even the existential leap of faith cannot resurrect this dead God after Auschwitz', said Richard Rubenstein.[16]

It is not too much to say that the author of Job drove the first nail into the coffin destined for theism, even though it was not until the nineteenth and twentieth centuries (as we have seen in chapter 4) that 'God' finally expired. The reason why Job's attack on the morality of God did not lead more immediately to further questioning of theism is that the people of Israel began to embrace a quite new way of solving the problem of the suffering righteous. They began to transfer the time of vindication from this life to an era beyond death.

In the last two centuries before the Christian era Israelite thought (influenced by Zoroastrianism) began to accept the concept of a Last Judgment at the end of time and hence after most people had been long dead. By the time of the book of Daniel it had become quite explicit, as we see in the words, 'And many of those who sleep in the dust of the earth shall awake, some to everlasting life and some to shame and everlasting contempt'.[17] This belief was promoted by the Pharisees but rejected by the Sadducees. Among Christians this belief eventually evolved into the supernatural structure of heaven, purgatory, and hell (as already referred to in chapter 7). There is no need here to describe the rise and fall of Christian eschatology,[18] but what does need to be pointed out is that it all began in the attempt to re-establish the moral nature of the universe and hence defend the morality of a divine Creator.

Until the Babylonian Exile any natural desire for immortality which Israelites might have experienced was sufficiently met by the logical consequences of community thinking: first, one lived on in one's offspring and second, the people of Israel lived on indefinitely even if the individual Israelite did not. The mortality of the human condition began to loom as a problem only in the post-exilic shift from community thinking to individual thinking. The problem was exacerbated by the breakdown of the dogma that good and evil behaviour always reap their due reward within the limits of this life. The transfer of divine judgment to a post-mortem experience alleviated this problem. What Job asked for was not eternal life but moral justice. He expressed the hope that even after he had died, a *goel* (advocate) would stand up for him before God and press home his claim for moral justification.[19]

The sages had always affirmed the complete mortality of the human condition, as did Israel as a whole; they did not regard departure to Sheol (the mythical underworld of the dead) as in any sense a 'life after death'. It was simply a euphemism for death; Job, in his opening speech, explained why it offered no hope. Except in the Wisdom of Solomon, the sages do not seem to have been greatly attracted to the idea of a post-mortem judgment as a solution to the morality of human existence.

This is particularly the case with the sage who was perhaps the greatest of them all in the pre-Christian period. We know him as Ecclesiastes; this is the Greek translation of *Qoheleth*, a word that can mean either 'the Preacher' or 'the Collector of wisdom'. Qoheleth chose to write as if he were the re-incarnation of Solomon. He not only rejected the dogmas of the early wisdom tradition, which Job had already so brilliantly challenged, but he also held up to critical enquiry the pursuit of wisdom itself. He conceded that wisdom was more profitable than folly but then noted that, in spite of this, death comes to the wise man in the same way it does to the fool — and even to the animals.

He became disillusioned with all human endeavour to solve problems and to produce lasting achievements. It became the first of the two themes which keep reappearing as refrains in his book. We are familiar with it in the KJV as: 'Vanity of vanities, everything is vanity!' The Hebrew word *hevel* refers to the human breath visible to our eyes on a frosty morning; it is so unsubstantial that it disappears into thin air before our very eyes. Qoheleth used the word to express his conviction that wherever one turned, and whatever one did, one could find nothing solid or permanent. Trying to create something lasting he found to be as futile as chasing the wind; everything eventually passes away and disappears. 'Emptiness, emptiness, everything's empty', he said.

Having followed several careers and observed a number of truths about society and the world, Qoheleth arrived at an existentialist attitude toward life. He acknowledged that 'God had made everything beautiful in its time' and had given humankind plenty to occupy itself. God had even created human beings in such a way that their minds can contain (in imagination) the whole world of space and time. Yet the work of God remains hidden and can lead humans to adversity as easily as to prosperity.[20] These reflections kept leading him back to his second theme: 'the best thing that a person can do in life is to eat and drink and find enjoyment in what he does'.[21]

More than any priest, prophet or even sage before him, Qoheleth examined the nature of human existence. He asked such basic questions as: What does it mean to be human? In the absence of any certainty or permanence, how can one get the best out of life? In doing so he raised the pursuit of Wisdom to a higher level. True sages had to do more than collect gems of wisdom, select the best, and pass them on to their students. Wisdom could not be stored and it was vain or empty to think that it could be. One had to walk the path of wisdom for oneself rather than simply inherit it from others without having to think for oneself. The role of the sage was not to provide instant wisdom for the foolish and unlearned; the words of the sage were to be like a sharp goad[22] forcing the hearer to shake off his complacency and pursue wisdom for himself.

There is a certain modernity about the words of Qoheleth, as even a fairly orthodox scholar such as Ben Witherington III has noted.[23] I encountered surprising evidence of how strikingly relevant Ecclesiastes is to our time when, some thirty-five years ago, I preached a sermon on Ecclesiastes at a university service which marked the opening of the academic year. I tried to show how it reflected many of our modern problems, mainly because it was written at a time like ours, when the traditional religious dogmas were no longer convincing. I agreed with Ecclesiastes that we are mortal creatures who have no immortal souls but who nevertheless face the quandary of how best to live out our short span of life within this amazing universe. And to meet this challenge we have no infallible source of knowledge or wisdom to give us all the answers.

The next morning all Hell broke loose. Church leaders, on being asked by journalists what they thought of the sermon, appeared extremely shocked. A fundamentalist professor of Classics complained that I had chosen to preach on Ecclesiastes when I should have selected one of the many encouraging Gospel messages to be found in the Bible. The furore led to the publication of the full text of the sermon in all the metropolitan newspapers. That gave rise to widespread public debate on the sensitive issue of what happens to us when we die. In every newspaper and magazine in the country, even as far afield as Australia, there appeared articles and editorials on the issue. The voice of Ecclesiastes had struck a very tender nerve.

The humanist tradition of Hebrew Wisdom did not look to Yahweh to deliver people by miraculous interventions in either nature or human history. It taught people to pursue the way of Wisdom and it relegated God to the role of an impersonal creative force which had shaped the world to be as it was. The world was awe-inspiring, it could not be changed, and reverence for its structure was the beginning of wisdom. All these facts placed the sage in considerable tension with the loyal Yahwist of Israelite tradition, whether prophet, priest, or royalist. This tension is not unlike that which occurred very much later between Erasmus (the Renaissance humanist) and Luther (the Protestant champion of divine grace). It is the same tension, amounting at times to animosity, which exists today between secular humanists and fundamentalists.

What happened to Hebrew humanism after Qoheleth? Did his somewhat pessimistic view of life lead humanism down a blind path? That is how many have interpreted him. The book of Jesus ben Sirach and the Wisdom of Solomon (both of which were probably written after Ecclesiastes) led Wisdom back into the main-stream of Israelite culture. They fashioned a rapprochement with the Torah tradition and the prophets similar to the long-standing alliance between the Kingdom stream and the prophets. This is reflected in the mini-epic, Sirach 44–50, where wisdom is associated with all the crucial events in Israel's history.

In the Wisdom of Solomon the association with main-stream Judaism is even more marked in that, in strong contrast with Qoheleth, there is a strong reaffirmation of trust in the national God of Israel.[24] At the same time, however, it shows the influence of Greek thought in spite of having been written by a loyal and orthodox Jew. In a number of places[25] it reflects Plato's doctrine of the immortality of the soul, a notion quite foreign to the Israelite tradition. It was this, rather than the new Jewish belief in resurrection and Last Judgment which led him to write: 'The souls of the righteous are in the hand of God, and no torment will ever touch them. In the eyes of the foolish they seemed to have died and their departure was thought to be an affliction . . . but they are at peace. For though in the sight of men they were punished, their hope is full of immortality'.[26]

These last two books of Wisdom show how the Diaspora Jews, living in a Hellenistic environment, were trying to find a way of retaining their identity while at the same time entering into dialogue with the dominant culture. The living voice of the prophet was no longer heard and to some extent was being replaced by apocalyptic writers. Too rigid adherence to the Torah led to a life-less legalism. Because of its humanistic base the Wisdom stream was well equipped to carry the Jewish tradition forward in the wider, multi-cultural environment. We shall now see how it did it.

Chapter Nine

Was Jesus the wise man par excellence?

t the beginning of the Christian era the Jewish cultural tradition was in a vigorous state, having recovered from the near death-blow of the Babylonian Exile. Geographically, the Jewish Diaspora had spread quite widely and Jewish culture was manifesting itself in a variety of diverse forms. It is interesting to observe what happened to its four main streams. The Kingdom stream provided the basis for Christianity, not only because the teaching of Jesus revolved around the Kingdom theme but also because Jesus himself was soon being acclaimed as the awaited Messianic ruler. Rabbinic Judaism, on the other hand, largely abandoned the prophetic and kingdom streams after the Romans destroyed the Jerusalem Temple in 70 C.E. and focused its attention more than ever on the Torah. Some centuries later, the prophetic tradition was revived by Muhammad, who not only acknowledged all the earlier prophets from Moses to Jesus, but claimed to be the last of the prophets, with the Qur'an being the final revelation.

So much for three streams of Jewish culture but what happened to the Wisdom stream? It apparently became the Cinderella in all three religions of Israelite origin, even though in some respects, it could claim to be as old, if not older, than its rival and more successful sisters. In view of the long neglect of the Wisdom literature in the Christian Bible, that is how it seemed until quite recently. But just as Cinderella, hidden in obscurity though she was, finally proved to be the person the prince was looking for, so the Wisdom stream is at last coming to the fore, having been rediscovered in the most unlikely place.

Many New Testament scholars now claim that Jesus of Nazareth was primarily a sage who raised the Wisdom stream to new heights. Such a claim implies that Christianity originated not in the Kingdom stream, nor even in the prophetic stream, but in the Wisdom stream. If this is true, the origins and nature of Christianity have to be completely re-evaluated.

The reason why Christianity's Wisdom roots were so long lost to view is that at a very early stage Christian attention shifted from the message to the messenger. It turned from what Jesus taught about the Kingdom to what Christians were proclaiming about Jesus as the King (Messiah). Then, as Christian thought rapidly evolved within Hellenistic culture in the early centuries, the original Jewish Jesus became completely obscured by the cosmic figure of Christ. This was largely at the instigation of Paul who, on his own admission, had never met Jesus.

To be sure, Jewish scripture continued to be the Christian Bible, and Christians still drew from it. They portrayed the Christ figure as the culmination of the whole cultural tradition of Israel, and recorded him as saying — 'I have come not to abolish the law and the prophets, but to fulfil them'.[1] First, he was seen as the new Moses, delivering humanity from slavery to the Devil just as the first Moses led Israel out of slavery to the Egyptians; this is reflected in Matthew's Gospel, where the Sermon on the Mount parallels the Ten Commandments received by Moses on Mt Sinai. Then he was seen as the new High Priest who, in sacrificing himself, had made the Mosaic sacrificial system redundant; this is one of the themes of the Epistle to the Hebrews.[2] Thirdly, by drawing upon the messianic tradition, which went all the way back to the Israelite Golden Age of the Kingdom of David, Christ was honored as the King of kings and Lord of lords. This is why Christian theologians through the ages loved to expound the role of (Jesus) Christ as Prophet, Priest, and King. Today it seems a tragic irony that the historical Jesus' actual role — that of being a Hebrew Sage — was completely ignored and lost from sight.

But what are the reasons for claiming that Jesus was a Sage?

To begin with, it should be noted that such a possibility could not be seriously contemplated until the modern deconstruction of the traditional understanding of Jesus Christ, which occurred in the last two centuries and was briefly sketched in chapter 7. This deconstruction has been taking place within the academic world and is still largely rejected or ignored in the ecclesiastical world. In the churches it is still commonly accepted without question that Jesus himself claimed to be the Messiah, the Saviour, the Way, the Truth, and the Life. These self-assertions on his part are still often defended in popular debate by arguing, 'If Jesus was not the person he claimed to be, he was either mad or bad. Jesus was clearly neither insane nor a hoaxer. Therefore he was what claimed to be'. This argument became invalid as soon as modern scholarship discovered when and how the Gospels came to be written.

Intense biblical study has shown fairly convincingly that Jesus did not make any of these assertions about himself. The claims were first made by the early Christians, who themselves composed many of the words that the Gospels placed in the mouth of Jesus. This was not an act of deception but simply the kind of thing that happens in oral tradition. (All good Sunday School teachers do it frequently, as they try to develop and make interesting for their classes a story which the Bible tells in only a few verses.) Jesus, it now seems, did not talk much about himself at all; rather he talked about the Kingdom of God — a topic never even mentioned in the later creeds.

When the roles of prophet, priest, and king were removed, the first fact that came to light was that Jesus was in no sense a divine figure but was truly human in every way. The Jesus who has been rediscovered by biblical scholars in the last two centuries turns out to have been a charismatic teacher and healer, about whom we know all too little. Only in the last two or three decades have we been drawn a little closer to the original Jesus, largely through the work of the Fellows of the Jesus Seminar. It is now eminently reasonable to conclude that rather than being a king, priest, or even prophet, Jesus stood in the wisdom tradition more than anything else. It has led Robert Funk to say, not only that 'Jesus is one of the great sages of history'[3] but that 'Jesus is also a secular sage. His parables and aphorisms all but obliterate the boundaries separating the sacred from the secular'.[4]

This discovery rests to a large extent on the work done in connection with a hypothetical document called Q. This term stands for a written Source (*Quelle,* in German) which no longer exists as an independent document but which was hypothesised as long ago as 1838 to explain why Matthew and Luke share about 235 verses of common material in addition to the material which they both have clearly taken from Mark. If this hypothesis is correct, it not only solves the problem of how the Synoptic Gospels are related to one another but it throws surprising new light on the early Christian movement.

Q primarily consists of sayings of Jesus and is often now referred to as 'The Sayings Gospel'. Of course Q may have been larger than what has survived in both Luke and Matthew, but it evidently did not report any of the acts of Jesus; if it had, they would most likely have shown up in the two Gospels which used it. Since Q thus appears to be the earliest written Gospel, and since it is silent about the vicarious death and supposed resurrection of Jesus, we may reasonably infer that what chiefly concerned the earliest Christian movement was Jesus' message. In other words it saw Jesus primarily as a teacher, possibly even a sage.

What has survived of Q in Matthew and Luke has now become part and parcel of the totality of sayings that the four Gospels attribute to Jesus. In its attempt to recover what Jesus actually said, the Jesus Seminar studied all extant written sources from the ancient world and did not restrict itself to the canonical Gospels. The Fellows assembled some five hundred items, many of them occurring more than once. This data base for establishing the teaching of Jesus, along with the Seminar's conclusions, has been published as *The Five Gospels, What did Jesus Really Say?*

In the days when it was naively assumed that everything attributed to Jesus in the Bible actually came from his lips, it was a not uncommon practice to print these sayings in red. This gave the Jesus Seminar the idea of presenting its findings in such a way that the general reader can immediately see which of the recorded sayings of Jesus are most likely to be judged genuine in the light of modern scholarship. As the Fellows were doing their painstaking work over several years, they employed a simple voting procedure to reveal where the consensus lay and translated the results into a convenient color coding in the book just mentioned. Those sayings of Jesus judged most likely to be genuine are in red; those very possibly genuine, but perhaps somewhat modified, are in pink; those judged unlikely but perhaps related to something genuine are in grey; while those which definitely did not originate with Jesus appear in black. (In what follows we shall be drawing almost exclusively from those appearing in red or pink.)

The first thing to note about this restricted data base is that all the long discourses in the Fourth Gospel have disappeared; they are the ones in which Jesus speaks about himself, his mission, and his relationship with God the Father. All the items left are found chiefly in two formats — short aphorisms and parables. Now that is very striking, for we observed in the last chapter that the recorded work of the Israelite sages started with collections of short pithy sayings or aphorisms and then moved to more extended tractates on a common theme, finally ending in complete books.

Let us now explore whether there is any discernible relationship between the sayings of Jesus and those attributed to the earlier Jewish sages. We shall look first at the aphorisms. Whereas the sages consistently used two-line couplets, the aphorisms of Jesus were chiefly one-liners. (Of course, one has to allow for the fact that some element of the original format may have been lost, not only in oral transmission but also in translation from Aramaic to Greek.) On the other hand, as we have found in Ecclesiastes, there was already a strong tendency to shift from verse couplets to prose.

That there is a similarity in expression between Jesus and the sages may be illustrated by the following examples:

1. Ecclesiastes: What does a man gain by all the toil at which he toils under the sun?[5]
   Jesus: For what will it profit a man, if he gains the whole world and forfeits his life?[6]
2. Ecclesiastes: What is crooked cannot be made straight, and what is not there cannot be counted.[7]
   Jesus: And which of you by being anxious can add one cubit to his span of life?[8]
3. Ecclesiastes: The wise man has his eyes in his head, but the fool walks in darkness; and yet I perceived that one fate comes to all of them.[9]
   Jesus: God causes the sun to rise on the bad and the good, and sends rain on the just and the unjust.[10]

14

4. Sirach: Be content with little or much and you will not hear reproach for your sojourning.[11]
Jesus: Stay at that one house, eating and drinking whatever they provide. Whenever you enter a town and they welcome you, eat whatever is set before you.[12]
5. Sirach: Every creature loves its like, and every person his neighbour; all living beings associate by species, and a man clings to one like himself.[13]
Jesus: Tell me, if you love those who love you, why should you be commended for that? Even the toll collectors do as much, don't they?[14]

When it comes to the parables, long regarded as the most distinctive form of the teaching of Jesus, there may at first seem to be more contrast. Yet we need to remember that the Wisdom literature expressed many of its couplets in what it called a *mashal* or parable.

1. Proverbs: A man without self-control is like a city broken into and left without walls.[15]
Jesus: The kingdom of God is like leaven which a woman took and concealed in fifty pounds of flour until was all leavened.[16]
2. Proverbs: He who oppresses the poor to increase his own wealth, or gives to the rich, will only come to want.[17]
Jesus: It's easier for a camel to squeeze through a needle's eye than for a wealthy person to get into God's domain.[18]

Ecclesiastes even has a little story about a wise man, which is remarkably like the parables of Jesus:

Ecclesiastes: There was a little city with few men in it; and a great king came against it and besieged it, building great siegeworks against it. But there was found in it a poor wise man, and he by his wisdom delivered the city. Yet no one remembered that poor man. But I say that wisdom is better than might, though the poor man's wisdom is despised, and his words not heeded.[19]

Compare that with Jesus:

Once there was a judge in this town who neither feared God nor cared about people. In that same town was a widow who kept coming to him and demanding, 'Give me a ruling against the person I'm suing'. For a while he refused; but eventually he said to himself, 'I'm not afraid of God and I don't care about people, but this widow keeps pestering me. So I'm going to give her a favorable ruling, or else she'll keep coming back until she wears me down'.[20]

When the Jesus Seminar ranked the recorded sayings of Jesus according to authenticity one of the criteria it used was originality. This meant that material very similar to that found elsewhere in Judaism, and particularly material from the wisdom stream, tended to be placed in the grey or black categories. But if Jesus properly belongs within the tradition of the sages, then we would expect some overlap between what he said and what the sages before him had said. And the parallels are evident; for example, compare the following:

1. Jesus: Don't pass judgment, so you won't be judged. Don't forget, the judgment you hand out will be the judgment you get.[21]
Sirach: Before making judgment examine yourself, and in the hour of your being assessed you will find forgiveness.[22]

2. Jesus: Do not lay up for yourselves treasures on earth where moth and rust consume and where thieves break in and steal but lay up for yourselves treasure in heaven.[23]
Sirach: Lose your silver for the sake of a brother or a friend, and do not let it rust under a stone and be lost. Lay up treasure according to the commandments of the Most High and it will profit you more than gold.[24]

Even the term 'Kingdom of God', which is so distinctive of the teaching of Jesus, was not wholly original, for we find it in Wisdom:

When a righteous man fled from his brother's anger wisdom guided him on straight paths; she showed him the kingdom of God and gave him knowledge of holy things.[25]

Up to this point we have been trying to show the relationship between the teaching of Jesus and the Wisdom stream in the Jewish cultural tradition. We have already noted that Jesus spoke in aphorisms as the sages did, and he frequently used the parable form just as they did the *mashal*. But he did a great deal more than that and to this we must now turn. Jesus, developed the prose parable into a unique new genre. In the quality and depth of his teaching Jesus lifted the Wisdom stream to a new level. In some respects Jesus is closest to Qoheleth in that both deal with issues of human existence, issues common to all humans irrespective of their cultural differences. The chief difference between the two is that Qoheleth, while encouraging people to enjoy life, tends to succumb to melancholy whereas Jesus, while acknowledging the frustrations and enigmas of life, always looked into the future with faith and hope.

Nowhere does this show up more clearly than in the humor of Jesus. We take the Gospels so seriously that we often fail to appreciate how Jesus used humor to great effect. Here are some examples:

> It's easier for a camel to squeeze through the eye of a needle than for a wealthy man to get into God's domain![26]

(In long dissertations and in many sermons people have tried to rationalize what Jesus said, instead of taking it to be the ridiculously amusing, yet provocative, statement that it is.)

Why do you notice the sliver in your friend's eye, but overlook the log of timber in your own? How can you say to your friend, 'Let me get the sliver out of your eye', when there is that piece of timber in your own? You phony, first take the log out of your own eye and then you'll see well enough to remove the sliver from your friend's eye'.[27]

> If anyone sues you for your coat, let him have your cloak as well.[28]

(In those days most people wore only two garments. The modern equivalent would be something like this, 'If any one insists on taking the shirt off your back as security, give him your underpants as well'. There would have been howls of laughter.)

Let us now compare the chief recurring theme of Qoheleth with the words of Jesus:

> Qoheleth: 'the best thing that a person can do in life is to eat and drink and find enjoyment in what he does'.[29]

Jesus not only so enjoyed food, wine and good company that he was accused of being 'a glutton and a drunk and crony of toll collectors and sinners'[30] but he did so with a carefree spirit. His advice was,

Don't fret about your life — what you're going to eat and drink, or about your body — what you're going to wear. There is more to living than food and clothing, isn't there? Take a look at the birds of the sky: they don't plant or harvest, or gather into barns. Yet your heavenly Father feeds them. You're worth more than they, aren't you? Can any of you add one hour to life by fretting about it? Why worry about clothes? Notice how the wild lilies grow: they don't slave and they never spin. Yet let me tell you, even Solomon at the height of his glory was never decked out like one of them. If God dresses up the grass in the field, which is here today and tomorrow is thrown into the oven, won't God care for you even more, you who don't take anything for granted?'[31]

We are so used to reading the highly developed portraits of Jesus in the Gospels that, even when we try to isolate the original words of Jesus as we are now doing, we still tend to read them in the light of those later developments. Thus we miss such points of similarity between Qoheleth and Jesus as it is still possible to uncover. The difference between the two is not so much in their understanding of the nature of human existence as in the proper attitude to take towards it. In this respect it may be said that for Qoheleth the proverbial milkbottle was half empty but for Jesus it was half full.

Qoheleth, as we have seen, argued that 'the best thing that a person can do in life is to eat and drink and find enjoyment in what he does'. Jesus also enjoyed life and encouraged others to do the same. This is implied in his saying, 'leave it to the dead to bury their own dead'.[32] It is also reflected in the much later Johannine words, 'I have come that people may have life and have it abundantly';[33] and that is surely true to the spirit of Jesus even though there he is portrayed as the doorway through which to pass in order to live the abundant life instead of being simply the one who encourages people to live life to the full.

We can now say with some confidence that Jesus never spoke of himself as divine. But neither did he have much to say about God as a personal being. He referred to God in much the same way as the sages did. God-language was part of Israelite and later Jewish culture. We may compare it with the way Shakespeare refers to God. For Shakespeare God-language was simply part of traditional English culture; his own religious attitude reflected that of the Renaissance humanists more than that of the traditional church. He was no doctrinaire atheist and yet he was almost exclusively concerned with the human condition rather than with God. So were the Jewish sages, and so was Jesus.

Indeed, Jesus did not say much about God; rather, he talked about the **kingdom** of God. When we read the parables of the kingdom, we find they are pointing to, and sometimes describing, human attitudes to life, the nature of human relationships, and the kind of society which we should be striving to build.

Jesus taught people to look into the future with faith and hope, but he never encouraged people to let God take over their lives and make all their decisions for them, as do some evangelicals today. Rather, he taught people to take full responsibility for their lives and to make every effort to make the right decision in every situation. He said, 'Struggle to get in through the narrow door; I'm telling you, many will try to get in but won't be able'.[34]

In order to make the right decision and to exercise responsibility one must have some measure of freedom of choice. Jesus acknowledged this freedom. Not only did he himself manifest a surprising measure of freedom in relation to the culture and the religious laws of the day, but he encouraged others to do the same. Take for example what he said about sabbath observance — one of the basic Ten Commandments. 'The sabbath day was created for Adam and Eve, not Adam and Eve for the sabbath day. So the son of Adam [i.e. humankind] lords it over even the sabbath day'.[35]

There is almost universal agreement that the most important theme in the teaching of Jesus is brotherly love, the subject of perhaps his best known parable — that of the Good Samaritan. Christians have long taught that the two most important commandments given by Jesus are these: 'Love the Lord your God with all your heart and soul and mind and strength. And love your neighbour as yourself'. But they too often forget that Jesus did not formulate these; as a good Jew, he was simply quoting from the Hebrew Bible, where these words are found, respectively, in Deuteronomy 6:5 and Leviticus 19:18.

The place where Jesus was wholly original was in the now famous words — 'Love your enemies'.[36] This was a quite revolutionary statement and it still is. He expounded it further:

> Tell me, if you love those who love you, why should you be commended for that? Even the toll collectors do as much, don't they?

> Don't react violently against the one who is evil: when someone slaps you on the right cheek, turn the other as well. When anyone forces you to go for one mile, go an extra mile. Give to the one who begs from you; don't turn away the one who tries to borrow from you.[37]

Christians have long treasured and commended such behaviour but have found it exceedingly difficult to execute. I write these words less than a week after the terrorist attacks on New York and Washington, which have shocked the world. How does the predominantly Christian nation of the United States react? There are very urgent calls for vengeance on the enemy. The allegiance of United States citizens to the Christian faith is being sorely tested by how they now respond. Jesus taught that violence achieves nothing, whether it comes from the terrorists or from the response to the terrorists. This most basic teaching of Jesus the sage could not be more relevant than it is today in this era of the globalizing of humankind. It was just as relevant to the violence and tensions being experienced under Roman rule in the Holy Land of Jesus' day.

Jesus himself met a violent death at the hands of the Romans. That was the tragic irony which sparked the rise of the Christian movement, namely that the man who initiated the path of non-violence should have suffered the cruel death of crucifixion. His followers later portrayed Jesus as saying from the cross, 'Father forgive them for they don't know what they are doing.'[38] Was that death to be the end of the wisdom stream which Jesus had raised to such heights? Not straight away!

The New Testament writing that is closest to the Wisdom stream is the Epistle of James. We do not know who wrote it but there is an ancient tradition, later espoused by Jerome (c. 340–420), that it originated with James, the brother of Jesus and the leader of the Jerusalem Christians. This suggests that it reflects the sentiments embraced by the primitive Jewish Christians. This in turn suggests that its chief themes may be closer to the teaching **of** Jesus than the beliefs **about** Jesus contained in the Pauline and Johannine writings. It is instructive to observe how clearly James reflects the wisdom tradition.

The chief theme of James is the living of the 'good life' and this is said to be achieved by the pursuit of wisdom. Further, wisdom is regarded as a spiritual gift which originates with God, much as the sages had always asserted. 'If any of you lacks wisdom', writes James at the outset, 'let him ask God, who gives to all people generously and without reproaching, and it will be given him'.[39]

But James makes a sharp distinction between the wisdom which is a spiritual gift and the pseudo-wisdom of the arrogant know-all.

> Who is wise and understanding among you? By his good life let him show his works in the meekness of wisdom. But if you have bitter jealousy and selfish ambition in your hearts, do not boast and be false to the truth. This wisdom is not such as comes from above, but is earthly, unspiritual, devilish . . . But the wisdom from above is first pure, then peaceable, gentle, open to reason, full of mercy and good fruits, without uncertainty and insincerity'.[40]

Also in harmony with the sages and with Jesus is the acknowledgement of the uncertain and unpredictable vagaries of life.

> Come now, you who say 'Today or tomorrow we will go into such and such a town and spend a year there and trade and get gain'; whereas you do not know about tomorrow. What is your life? For you are a mist that appears for a little time and then vanishes. Instead you ought to say, 'If the Lord wills, we shall live and we shall do this or that' As it is, you boast in your ignorance.[41]

It should be observed that James, like the sages, does not encourage his readers to think that they are immortal or that divine providence will preserve them from harm or misfortune. The reference to the Lord could just as readily be replaced by 'fate' without any real change in meaning.

Another early Christian book which is in keeping with the wisdom stream is the *Didache* (The Teaching of the Lord to the Gentiles through the Twelve Apostles). This document long lay lost and was rediscovered as recently as 1873. It is known to have been widely used in the ancient church; Athanasius (c.296–373) recommended its use and Clement of Alexandria (c. 150–215) regarded it as holy scripture.

The Didache begins thus: 'There are two ways: a Way of Life and a Way of Death, and the difference between these two Ways is great'[42] Not only do these words immediately catch the spirit of the wise men of Israel but we find frequent use of the term 'way' in Proverbs as in 'Her (i.e. Wisdom's) ways are ways of pleasantness, and all her paths are peace'.[43] Moreover, it is now widely believed that the earliest name for what we now call Christianity was simply 'The Way'.[44]

What was the substance of this Way of Life? — 'Thou shalt love first the Lord thy Creator, and secondly thy neighbour as thyself; and thou shalt do nothing to any man that thou wouldst not wish to be done to thyself'. There follow many more specific instructions about living a moral and circumspect life but there are absolutely no references to the Gospel of the Saviour Christ as proclaimed by Paul. And this is in spite of the fact that the second half of the Didache gives instruction on church practice concerning baptism, prayer, the eucharist, and charismatic experiences.

From the second century onwards, the stream of human wisdom, so wonderfully exemplified by Jesus of Nazareth and reflected in James, in the Didache, and to some extent in Matthew's Gospel, began to fade into insignificance within the developing Christian movement. It became completely overshadowed by the Pauline Gospel of the Saviour Christ, crucified, risen, and glorified.

From the time of Paul, and perhaps even earlier, the Christian Gospel was assumed to be the proclamation of the death and resurrection of Jesus Christ as the unique cosmic event which brought divine salvation to humankind. (Just how the Easter faith of the resurrection of Christ arose was discussed briefly in chapter 6.[45]) This Pauline Gospel soon displaced the wisdom elements prominent in both the teaching of Jesus and in the Jerusalem church. Indeed Paul, who is known to have been strongly critical of Peter and the Jerusalem church on other grounds, had some quite scathing words to say about wisdom, equating it with the Greeks.

> Where is the wise man? . . . Has not God made foolish the wisdom of the world? . . . The world did not know God through wisdom . . . For Jews demand signs and Greeks seek wisdom but we preach Christ crucified, a stumbling block to the Jews and foolishness to Gentiles, but to those who are called, both Jews and Greeks, Christ the power of God and the wisdom of God. For the foolishness of God is wiser than men.[46]

No wonder Martin Luther, well schooled in the theology of Paul and Augustine, despised the Epistle of James, discounted all human endeavour as encouraged by the wisdom stream, and taught Protestants to put their trust in 'justification by faith alone'.

Only with the advent of the modern, secular and humanist world and the realisation that there is no Divine being in heaven to control human affairs and put all things right is the long neglected stream of wisdom tradition at last coming into its own. As we noted earlier, the Wisdom writings of the Old Testament have been called the books of Hebrew humanism. After nearly two thousand years, we are perhaps now ready to receive the guidance and encouragement that can come to us from the voiceprints of Jesus, the man of wisdom par excellence.

Chapter Ten

Why Christianity must become non-theistic

s we return to the question with which this book began — 'Can Christianity exist without belief in God?' — it behooves us to summarise what followed. We are now in a position to see that the form of the question is too ambiguous to be given a valid answer. First, Christianity can best be understood not as something fixed and absolute but as a broad and changing stream of living culture which reflects in some way the originating influence of Jesus of Nazareth. Second, the term 'God' not only has a long and complex history, but in modern times it has either ceased to be used at all or is being used in such a variety of ways that it has become a very confusing word.

If we think of God as 'a superhuman person regarded as having power over nature and human fortunes',[1] we are using a descriptive definition. But if we take 'God' to refer to the highest values which motivate us, then we are using a functional definition. As the theologian Gordon Kaufman has pointed out, even in a secular world the term 'God' can still have a useful function for us as 'an ultimate point of reference'. This leads him to say in his book *In Face of Mystery*, 'To believe in God is to commit oneself to a particular way of ordering one's life and action. It is to devote oneself to working towards a fully humane world within the ecological restraints here on planet Earth, while standing in piety and awe before the profound mysteries of existence.'[2] If indeed that defines 'belief in God' few would wish to call themselves atheists.

It must be conceded, however, that most people in the past assumed the descriptive definition and took the term 'God' to be the name of an objective, living, and thinking being. They believed this unseen spiritual being not only to have created the world but also to be still in control of it. Many followed the practice of communicating with this God on personal terms and expected to have their prayers answered. As we have seen in chapter 4, this understanding of God is referred to philosophically as theism. To avoid ambiguity, then, let us reformulate the original question to read 'Can Christianity exist without **theism**?' and hereafter so understand the phrase 'Christianity without God'.

In the first seven chapters I tried to show first, that Christianity does not really depend on theism and, secondly, that even in its origins Christianity was already moving towards the ultimate rejection of pure theism in its doctrine of the incarnation. So at the end of Chapter 7, I hauled in the two kites I had been flying.

As already noted in chapter 7, the final rejection of theism can be called humanism, although even this term also has a variety of shades of meaning. It is secular humanism which quite specifically denies reality to divine spiritual beings of any kind and as a consequence rejects 'acts of God', miracles, divine revelation, and all things supernatural. This humanism acknowledges that all of our values, concepts, and religions are of human origin. Orthodox Christians, by contrast, have usually assigned a lesser value to all things human and are today strongly opposed to such humanism. In view of this, it is somewhat ironic that they should take such delight in the doctrine of the incarnation (which means the enfleshment of God in human form).

It has been argued in this book that the modern secular world has evolved out of Western Christian culture, having been promoted by the Renaissance humanists, the Protestant Reformers, and free-thinking leaders of the Enlightenment. This evolution may be regarded as the natural result of taking the doctrine of the incarnation to its logical conclusion.

In chapter 8, therefore, we turned back to examine the long neglected Wisdom stream of the Hebraic legacy and to recover some of the early seeds of humanism. Since the Wisdom stream may be said to have reached a peak in the sage-like teachings of Jesus of Nazareth, it can be legitimately claimed that humanistic or non-theistic Christianity is not only a genuine heir to the Wisdom stream of ancient Israel but also that it is firmly grounded in the Jesus tradition. Whether one prefers to use the term 'humanistic Christianity', 'non-theistic Christianity', or simply 'post-Christianity' is a matter of personal choice; we need not be detained by a purely academic debate about the use of terms. What is important to understand is simply this: the modern secular, humanist, post-Christian world not only flowed out of traditional Christianity but manifests the continuing development of elements intrinsic to the Judeo-Christian tradition. For this reason, the modern secular and humanist world can legitimately be called 'Christianity without God'.

Having demonstrated how Christianity **can** exist without theism, let us now proceed to discuss why Christianity **must** henceforth 'take final leave of God'.[3] It must do so first, to continue along on the path to freedom on which it set forth; second, to be true to its own early development as expressed in the doctrines of the trinity and the incarnation; and third, for the ultimate salvation of humankind and of all life, on this planet.

Let us start with the pursuit of human freedom, which is one of the basic themes running through the whole of the Judeo-Christian cultural tradition. It began with the series of events known as the Exodus, when Moses led his people out of slavery in Egypt to reach a life of freedom in the land of Canaan. That long trek through the wilderness to freedom became a parable of human life itself for both Jews and Christians.

Furthermore, the Exodus tradition inspired many struggles for freedom; for even when freedom has been won, it can all too easily be lost. In the course of time the meticulous observance of the Mosaic tradition led to a new kind of slavery — enslavement to the written word of the law. At least, that is how the early Christians saw it, even though many of today's Jews would strongly deny that they find the legal prescriptions of the Torah burdensome.

The New Testament contrasts the somewhat carefree attitude of Jesus towards the Torah with that of the scribes and Pharisees. These strict observers of the law were accused of binding heavy burdens and placing them on men's shoulders.[4] Jesus initiated a new sense of freedom and demonstrated what it meant to be a free and responsible person. Not only did he himself repudiate strict observance of the sabbath and purity laws, but the author of the Fourth Gospel attributed to him the liberating proclamation, 'And you will know the truth and the truth will make you free'.[5]

As the earliest documents in the New Testament show, Paul battled hard to promote and safeguard this new life of freedom which was to characterise the Christian way. He urged his Galatian converts not to allow themselves to be drawn back into their former state of enslavement to the Torah. 'You were called to freedom', he exclaimed, and went on to say that 'The whole Torah is fulfilled in one word "You shall love your neighbour as yourself".' (This, incidentally, is a surprisingly humanistic statement to find in the otherwise theistic writings of Paul, and it has been traced back to his Jewish teacher Gamaliel).

But just as Jewish legalism had been seen by the early Christians as a form of slavery from which they needed to be freed, so in the course of time the power and authority of the ecclesiastical institution developed into another form of enslavement. That is just how the Augustinian monk Martin Luther experienced ecclesiastical discipline and why he broke free of it and opened up the way to the new freedom present within the Protestant movement. Luther likened life in the mediaeval church to that of the Jews in the Babylonian Exile and wrote a treatise on *The Babylonian Captivity of the Church.*

But the freedom won by Protestantism soon developed into another form of bondage — enslavement to the written word of the Bible. This has reached its most rigid form in modern fundamentalism. Thus both Jews and Christians have allowed themselves to become enslaved by their respective traditions, even though their common tradition is based on the theme of the journey towards freedom.

Indeed, until the Enlightenment (and even for a long time afterwards) human freedom was regarded in the Christian world as a dangerous phenomenon, an open door to civil unrest, rebellion, and social chaos. It was firmly believed that people were not meant to be free; rather they were created to be subject to authority — subject to God the Supreme Ruler, subject to the King (who ruled under God) and, finally, subject to the position in life that God had allotted to them. People were not even meant to be free to have their own thoughts, to say nothing of the lack of freedom to express them in speech. On the contrary, people were expected to think the thoughts prescribed by God through the Bible, thoughts that would win God's approval. Of course, church authorities determined what those thoughts were and also provided absolution for those who confessed how far they had strayed from right thinking.

Therefore the daring pioneers of the modern world who claimed the right to think for themselves were called free-thinkers. Today we are more and more becoming free-thinkers in the literal sense of that term, and we jealously guard the principles of free thought and free speech. Yet this world-shattering breakthrough in the area of human freedom was judged to be such a dangerous manifestation of hubris that pejorative associations accompany the term 'free-thought' to this day. The freedom of people to think for themselves, and subsequently to express their thoughts publicly, was the necessary prelude to the opening up of the modern world. It quickly led to a whole series of new emancipations, where the authorities of the past came under challenge.

First came the emancipation from absolute monarchy, a process which took an especially violent form in the French Revolution. Step by step everywhere in the Western world, absolute rule by hereditary monarchs was replaced by democratic self-rule, under which every person has, in theory at least, an equal say in the governing of society. Very few Christians, if any, would condemn democracy today, yet before the eighteenth century Christianity was wedded to the upholding of royal authority and even spoke of the 'divine right of kings'. The power structures in society, including those of class, were believed to have been ordained by God and any attempt to overthrow them was regarded as a direct assault on the divine prerogative. Democracy, accompanied by the breaking down of class divisions, has evolved out of the Christian West only in modern times.

Then came the affirmation of basic human rights. Up until that time the emphasis had been almost exclusively on the duties and responsibilities owed to higher authorities; humans had never been taught to believe they had any rights by virtue of being human. So appeal to human rights led, in turn, to the abolition of slavery, the rejection of racism, the emancipation of women, and the acceptance of homosexuals. All these emancipations evolved out of the Christian matrix and today are even sometimes referred to as Christian values. Yet each of these innovations has pitted the developing secular world against the entrenched dogmas of conventional Christianity. The Roman Catholic Church still jealously preserves the male character of the priesthood. Many churches are still in the process of coming to terms with the phenomenon of homosexuality. The emancipations already won, along with those still in the process of being achieved, have been made possible only because at the same time we have also been steadily emancipating ourselves from obedience to a supposed supernatural heavenly Father, whose revealed will was not to be questioned.

We have now reached the stage within the evolving stream of Christian tradition when to achieve the most mature state of personhood we must become emancipated from the last element of our cultural tradition which has the capacity to enslave us — namely, theism. We cannot be fully human until we experience the widest possible range of choices, and learn to take full responsibility for our choices in both action and thought. This we cannot do if we are forced to accept the beliefs of others as our own beliefs or if we have to conform to the dictates of an external commanding voice. Persons who are honest out of free choice, for example, are more ethically sensitive and more morally mature and responsible than those who act honestly only because they are ordered to do so by an external authority. Characteristic of the Second Axial Period is that the moral imperative which we experience in the human condition has been internalized. This does not make morality any less important than it was before, but it does make it possible for us to become more morally responsible persons.

Freedom from the commanding voice of a supposed divine authority is even more important now that we are in a position to realise that what our forbears took to be the divine voice, either in the Bible or in the church, turns out to be simply the voice of other humans like ourselves. When persons are elected as Popes, consecrated as bishops, or ordained as clergy, they remain as human and fallible as they were before. All church edicts are of human origin and open to error. The Protestant Reformers reached that conclusion and said so. 'All synods or councils since the apostles' time, whether general or particular, may err and many have erred; therefore they are not to be made the rule of faith or practice, but to be used as an help in both'.[6]

Since the modern revolution in understanding the Bible we are now able to go further than the Reformers and declare that the Bible also can err, and frequently does, for it was composed by humans. Inspiring though we may find the Bible in parts, it also transmits the errors and prejudices of those who wrote it. In the light of these discoveries about the origin of the Bible, it means that to retain the traditional view of the Bible's authority and inerrancy is to fall into the practice of idolatry.

The human origin of what was long taken to be divine does not prevent us from learning much of value from it, just as we still value the advice of our parents, peers, and teachers even after we have reached adulthood and learned to live our lives on their level. The reason why theism is now seen to be dangerous is that it added to purely human words a dimension of absolute authority which they did not deserve. It is this fact that so often caused the Inquisition in mediaeval times, and fundamentalists in modern times, to become irrational, dogmatic, and fanatical. To express it simply and somewhat crudely, the continuance of theism enables people unconsciously to project their own beliefs on to a divine authority and then attempt to impose them on their fellows, in the belief that in doing so they are simply obeying the divine imperative.

This damning feature of theism was first brought home to me at an international conference on 'God' in Hawaii in 1981. A South African scholar, Martin Prozesky, observed that 'Christianity had a disquieting ability to co-exist with or even encourage social evils like slavery and apartheid'.[7] He contended that traditional, orthodox theism with its belief in an almighty deity, especially of the conservative Calvinist kind that was dominant in white South Africa in the apartheid period, defined reality in strongly dominative social structures — owners controlling slaves, whites control-

ling blacks, men controlling women, humans controlling nature
and so on. Theism had the effect of sacralizing the dominative status quo and strongly discouraging any radical criticism of it on the
grounds that such criticism constituted a challenge to divine
authority.[8]

The further reason why theism must be abandoned is
because of the patriarchal and male-oriented character of the culture to which it led and which it continues to support. When the
Israelite prophets laid the foundation of (mono)theism they unfortunately left behind the gender complementarity which had existed
hitherto among the deities of the ancient religions. Previously the
divine figures had been conceived as gods and goddesses, who even
entered into romantic and procreative relationships with each
other. The Sky-Father had been complemented by the Earth-
Mother; and in many primitive myths of origin it was by their cop-
ulation that these two completed the creation process. The Israelite
prophets were so successful in their rejection of the goddesses as a
class that no word for goddess is to be found in the Hebrew Bible
and even the name of the Canaanite fertility goddess, Ashtoreth,
appears in an adulterated form, having had the vowels of the
Hebrew word meaning 'shame' inserted in it![9]

The absolute elimination of the Earth Mother (and other
goddesses) by the prophets had the effect of leaving all superhuman power in the hands of the Sky Father. He became the Father
Almighty ('Our Father in heaven'). The elimination of the chief
feminine deity, followed by the affirmation of the male deity as
supreme and unique, had the long-term effect of devaluing the
feminine gender and all the virtues associated with it. The Heavenly
Father of Jewish and Christian tradition evolved out of the Sky
Father who sent storms, lightning, and thunderbolts, and there is
much to suggest that he may also have been a god of war, since
one possible translation of 'The LORD of hosts' is 'The Lord of
armies'. In any case, 'Our Father in heaven' retained and even magnified the male nature of the earlier image. This was reflected in
the dominant and often over-bearing nature of male behaviour in
patriarchal society, while the softer virtues associated with mother-
hood and femininity came to be devalued.

It takes only a cursory glance at church tradition to see
how (male) monotheism has shaped Christian tradition and deter-

mined the male character of both church and society. Only males could become priests, exercise ecclesiastical rule, sing in church choirs, enter the holy precincts of the chancel and even utter their voices in church. 'Women should keep silence in the churches', decreed Paul, 'they are not permitted to speak but should be subordinate, as even the law says'.[10]

In the paving stones of Lincoln Cathedral in England there remains a line across the nave; I was told that in mediaeval times women could not approach the altar beyond that limit. Similarly, in the Jewish Temple the court of the women was situated outside the court of the men. In both Jewish and Christian traditions the natural physiological functions of the female body were thought to have the capacity to desecrate holy places and this meant that women had to be kept at a distance from 'the holy of holies'.

It was only to be expected, therefore, that one of the strongest challenges to traditional theism has been mounted by the modern feminist movement. For women to become truly liberated they must be free not only from male domination but also from a dominating male deity. The two go hand in hand, for as Mary Daly said, 'Where God is male, then the male is God'.[11] Contemporary theologians frequently defend theism by denying that male gender is at all applicable to the concept of God; hence prayers are sometimes addressed to 'Our divine Mother and Father'. Others regard such changes as no more than cosmetic and insist that for the true liberation of women, even more than of men, the traditional theism must be abandoned.

The new state of liberation of the human condition from divine control does not mean, however, that we are completely free to do what we like. Freedom must on no account be mistaken for license but must be exercised with full responsibility. When we reach adulthood and are given the key of the house to come and go as we please, with no questions to be asked by those who formerly controlled our youthful behaviour, we find there is a new burden of responsibility resting upon our shoulders. So it is with humankind's coming of age, as we enter this new and more permissive period. Some try to defend theism on the grounds that we are not yet ready for this new freedom. As we shall now see, however, this brings us to the third reason why theism must be abandoned.

We humans are earth creatures; we have slowly evolved on this planet as part of a biosphere which includes all the other forms of life. The earth has provided certain basic conditions which must be met by all earthly creatures if they are to survive as a species. We are bound by those parameters. For humans to be healthy we must be able to breathe fresh air, drink clean water, eat adequate food, and live in an environment not too different from that in which we have evolved. The more the environment changes from that in which a species has evolved, the more the health and behaviour of that species will show maladjustment. Its health will deteriorate and then it will die.

The survival of the human species on this planet is just as subject to the basic conditions supplied by the earth, as are all the other species. On the very day I find myself writing this (December 7, 2001), one hundred Nobel Laureates have just issued a brief but dire warning of the profound dangers facing the future of humankind. They declare that a secure future for humankind depends on immediate environmental and social reform. They point out that global warming (for which the affluent nations are largely responsible), coupled with the devastating power of modern weaponry (also a product of the West), is upsetting the fragile planetary ecology on which our existence depends. They believe the only hope for a long-term future for humankind lies in co-operative international action legitimized by democracy. They assert that we must learn to think in a new way.

So what was wrong with the old thinking? For centuries the Western world has encouraged us to believe that our future is in the hands of a benevolent and all-powerful God and that we have been placed here on earth to prepare for an eternal destiny elsewhere. Consequently we have focused our attention on the heavenly realm and devalued the natural physical world. What is more, we were encouraged by no less an authority than the Bible itself to believe that we 'have dominion over the fish of the sea, and over the birds of the air, and over the cattle, and over all the earth'.[12] And this was because we were made in the image of God and thus shared in his dominating power. In other words biblical theism encouraged us to exploit the earth.

That is why in 1973 the celebrated historian Arnold Toynbee went so far as to assert,

Some of the major maladies of the present day world — in particular the recklessly extravagant consumption of nature's irreplaceable treasures, and the pollution of those of them that man has not already devoured — can be traced back to a religious cause, and this cause is the rise of monotheism . . . Monotheism, as enunciated in the book of Genesis, has removed the age-old restraint that was once placed on man's greed by his awe. Man's greedy impulse to exploit nature used to be held in check by his pious worship of nature.[13]

Our distant pre-Axial ancestors were much more aware than we are that their continued existence on earth was dependent on the forces of nature. That is why they personified and deified these forces and tried to placate what they took to be their every whim. That is why they believed their own destiny to be in the lap of the gods, the most important of whom was Mother Earth.

One of the first modern thinkers to rediscover this vital significance of the ancient gods of nature was Ludwig Feuerbach. After having expounded what he took to be the true meaning of the incarnation in *The Essence of Christianity*[14] (which, as we have seen, spelled the end of theism), Feuerbach published a smaller and lesser-known book, *The Essence of Religion* (1846). In it he declared, 'The feeling of dependency in human beings is the basis of religion, but the object of this dependency, that upon which they are and feel themselves dependent, is originally nothing other than nature. *Nature* is the *first, original object of religion*, as is amply confirmed by the history of all religions and peoples'.[15]

The most pressing concerns of our dependence upon nature are very basic. They are largely the same as those we share with the other animals: the need for air, drink, food, shelter, survival. Built into every species, including the human species, are the instincts to survive and to procreate. The chief difference between us and the other animals is that, whereas they live much more by instinct and within a timeless present, we have evolved the capacity to think critically about the world of nature on which we depend, to be aware of a past and a future, to observe the phenomena of birth and death, and to experience what it means to be mortal. This was the starting-point from which our primitive human ancestors set out slowly and unconsciously to create human culture and all the various forms of religion in which they expressed their devotion.

We too must go that far back to establish the parameters of the new global and ecological culture and to create the forms of spirituality most appropriate to it. The need for pure air, clean water, nutritious food, adequate shelter, the regeneration of the species and the overcoming of all threats to human survival have once again become our most vital concerns. In our time these are the genuinely 'religious' issues to which we must 'devote' ourselves. For people of the third world, who have been living in a state of undernourishment for years, these must be even more clearly seen as the chief issues. Because their immediate concern is often to know where their next meal is coming from, these people can hardly be expected to show much interest in programmes of personal spiritual development, environmentalism, and international order, which either neglect or look beyond those basics.

Only people of the affluent countries are in a position to turn their attention to the wider problems — the care of the environment, the nurture of the ecology of the planet, the preservation of endangered species, the promotion of international peace, the fair sharing of the diminishing earth's resources, the curbing of the human birth rate, control and abolition of weapons of mass destruction, and a whole host of related topics. These are among the great religious issues of our age.

All those who, like the Nobel Laureates, are trying to make a positive response to these issues, have something in common with the Christian movement in the first century. The first Christians were also concerned with the future of the world. They were expecting a new world to break in upon them very soon — sometimes they called it the Kingdom of God, sometimes they spoke of it as 'a new heaven and new earth', and sometimes 'the return of Christ'. But they were definitely future-oriented.

The big difference between them and those who are future-oriented today is that they believed they simply had to wait patiently until God did it all for them in his own good time. Secular futurists today, however, know that the world's future is, as never before in human history, dependent upon us humans. Because the modern global, secular, humanist world stands in unbroken line of descent from the Christendom of the past, we can justifiably speak of this post-Christian dispensation as a further, but different, form of Christianity; it is now 'Christianity without God'. We humans must now shoulder full responsibility for the kind of future to be experienced by our children, grandchildren, and all later descendants; we can no longer shrug off our responsibility by transferring it to divine shoulders. Today we are called upon to make decisions (as in genetic modification) which previously were thought to be the sole prerogative of 'God'.

During the twentieth century that 'God' was slowly vanishing from the area of public consciousness and was no longer being appealed to by public bodies in times of pestilence, war, and drought, as once was the case. Even in churches it is rare to hear prayers beseeching God, say, to break the current drought; asking him to provide a fine day for the Sunday School picnic could be done only in jest. All public bodies, national and international, are now fully aware that humans themselves must solve the problems of our time and that there is no 'God' out there who can be appealed to when all else fails. The once public 'face of God' has been forced to retreat to the subjective consciousness of devout individuals and traditional church gatherings. 'God' has been privatized; what has remained public are the values inherited from the Christian past, values which continue to lead to fresh emancipations and new human ideals; and it is these values which constitute 'Christianity without God'.

The transition from Christendom to 'Christianity without God' is reflecting itself in common language. In three little books of a quite novel kind[16] Don Cupitt has made a study of the religiously interesting idioms now coming into colloquial English. He observed, for example, that as the word 'God' has been disappearing from public use, a whole host of little phrases focusing on 'life' (many of them new) have been coming into common usage, such as 'How's life been treating you lately?', 'Get a life!', 'That's the story of my life!' He suggests that the secularization of religion has had the effect of sacralizing life.

Cupitt also observed that the same change has been happening with our rituals. Funerals, for example, are ceasing to be events marking the departure of the deceased to their 'reward in heaven' and, instead, are becoming 'celebrations of a life', a life which is now ended and complete.

The visionary who wrote the Book of Revelation 'saw no temple in the 'New Jerusalem', and similarly there is no place for the institutional church (as we once knew it) in the society which lives by 'Christianity without God'. This should not surprise us. It is too little acknowledged that the authoritative and powerful ecclesiastical structure which dominated Europe for a thousand years owed more to the Roman Empire than it did to Jesus. That church developed to fill the power vacuum left by the Fall of Rome. Jesus certainly did not found it.

What is really distinctive about the social organisation of both Judaism and early Christianity is not a power structure but the simple gathering of people for mutual fellowship and support. That is the literal meaning of 'synagogue'. It named the new type of religious institution which arose during the Babylonian Exile to enable the Jews, then cut off from the Temple, to continue to associate together, to pray, and to study their heritage. The early church gathering (*ekklesia*) was modelled on the synagogue, as 'they devoted themselves to the apostles' teaching and fellowship, to the breaking of bread and the prayers'.[17]

In 'Christianity without God' there is still a place for rituals and festivals. They will celebrate everything we have come to value in human existence, such as the importance of healthy human relationships and the rich inheritance of human culture. This trend is already observable in the way Christians celebrate their chief ritual, known variously as Holy Communion, the Lord's Supper, or the Eucharist. For some time it has been interpreted less as the commemoration of a sacrifice offered on an altar to God and more as the sharing of a common meal round a table to celebrate the rich and sacred character of human fellowship. That indeed is how it actually began.

As humankind recovers a richer appreciation of how much our earthly life depends upon the conditions of the Earth itself, it will probably re-create the appropriate festivals to celebrate it. They will increasingly focus on and celebrate the natural processes which have brought life into being and which continue to sustain it. It is salutary to remember that the great annual Christian festivals (most of which Christianity inherited from Judaism) all originated as festivals celebrating the changing seasons of nature. The Feast of Pentecost originated as the early harvest festival. The Jewish Feast of Booths originated as the vintage festival. The Jewish festivals of Passover and Unleavened Bread, which later became the Christian

Easter, originated as early spring festivals celebrating the resurrection of nature to new life after the death of winter. The once widespread Christian celebration of Easter has largely disappeared except within churches. Much to the chagrin of traditional Christian clergy, the elements of Easter festivities which survive outside the churches are the Easter eggs and the Easter bunnies; ironically these point back to the very ancient spring festival out of which there developed the Jewish Passover and the Christian celebration of the death and resurrection of Jesus.

Christmas originated as a New Year festival celebrating the passing of the shortest day and the return of the sun. The festivity of Christmas is just as popular as ever but largely because it is already changing from being a commemoration of the birthday of the supposed Saviour of the world to a celebration of family life.

In 'Christianity without God' there is no place for the traditional figure of Christ as the divine Saviour. Yet there is certainly a place for Jesus the teacher, the man of wisdom, the one who revitalised the path to freedom. Of relevance to us is not the Jesus who was elevated into a mythical heaven but Jesus the fully human person who shared the tensions, enigmas, and uncertainties that we experience. It is Jesus who told stories which shocked people out of their traditional ways of thinking and behaving, who can free us from the mind-sets in which we have become imprisoned. The Jesus most relevant to us is he who provided no ready-made answers but by his tantalising stories prompted people to work out their own most appropriate answers to the problems of life. That is why the parables of the Good Samaritan and the Prodigal Son will be remembered long after the historic confessions and creeds have been forgotten.

Christianity can exist without God. Indeed, 'Christianity without God' has actually been in our midst for quite some time. It has been coming quietly, unheralded and unnoticed. It is rather like the way Jesus spoke of the arrival of the Kingdom of God: 'You won't be able to observe the coming of God's imperial rule. People are not going to be able to say, 'Look, here it is!' or 'Over there!' On the contrary, God's imperial rule is right there in your presence.[18]

It was 'Christianity without God' which made possible the series of emancipations mentioned above. Indeed, they may even be regarded as manifestations of the coming of the very Kingdom, of which Jesus spoke. Just as the early church saw evidence of the coming of the Kingdom in such events as 'the blind see, the lame walk, lepers are cleansed, the deaf hear',[19] so we may say that, though there is yet a long way to go, we can rejoice to see positive changes taking place:

> there is increasing personal freedom to think and to speak,
> the slaves are being freed,
> patriarchy is crumbling,
> homosexuals are free to 'come out',
> weapons of mass destruction are being widely condemned,
> racist attitudes are being overcome,
> equality of the sexes is being achieved,
> the disadvantaged are no longer being ignored,
> human worth and values are being increasingly honoured.

Notes

Chapter One

1. Anthony Freeman. See his book *God in Us*.
2. In a later chapter we shall discuss the history of the term.
3. Isaiah 55:11.
4. See Genesis 27.
5. See Genesis 11:1–9.
6. Genesis 3:8.
7. See, for example, *The Westminster Confession of Faith*, of 1647.
8. See the author's *New Idols for Old*.
9. Deuteronomy. 34:10.
10. 2 Timothy 3:16.

Chapter Two

1. Smith, *The Meaning and End of Religion*.
2. Harnack, *What is Christianity?*, p. 8.
3. Habakkuk 2:4.
4. Mark 5:34.
5. Smith, *Faith and Belief*, p. 12.
6. Hartshorne, *The Faith to Doubt*, p. 104.
7. Hebrews 11:8–10.
8. This was passed on to me orally by R.J.Zwi Werblowsky.
9. Acts 11:26.
10. Matthew 5:17.
11. Westminster Confession Faith XXV: V and VI (This is still the subordinate standard of Presbyterian churches).
12. For a much fuller discussion of this process, see the author's *Tomorrow's God*, Part III and *The World to Come*.

Chapter Three

1. John Calvin, *The Institutes of Christian Religion*, Book I, Chapter III, paragraph 1
2. For fuller discussion of the origin of language see the author's *Tomorrow's God*, chapter 1.
3. Genesis 2:7.
4. Ecclesiastes 12:7.
5. 2 Samuel 6:6–7.
6. For a full account of the Axial Period see the author's *Christian Faith at the Crossroads*.
7. Religion has been usefully defined as 'a total mode of the interpreting and living of life'. See the author's *Christian Faith at the Crossroads*, p. 4.
8. We know only the consonants of the name; the vowels are an attempt to restore the original ones.
9. Deuteronomy 5:7.
10. Jeremiah 7:6.
11. Isaiah 45:22.

12. See Isaiah 44:9–20.
13. Genesis 4:26.
14. See Exodus 3:13–15. Biblical scholars regard the etymology as somewhat contrived. Whereas Yahweh, when speaking of himself, will say 'I AM' (Ehyeh), humans need to refer to him in the third person and say 'HE IS', which, with some difficulty can be obtained out of 'Yahweh'.
15. Genesis 1:27.
16. John 1:1–4
17. See Jeremiah 18:1–6
18. See the author's Christian Faith at the Crossroads, p. xii.

Chapter 4
1. Macquarrie, *In Search of Deity*, p. 17.
2. For a much more extensive coverage see the author'*s Christian Faith at the Crossroads*, chaps. 3 and 4.
3. Kerr, ed., *A Compend of Luther's Theology*, p. 23 (italics added).
4. See John Macquarrie, *In Search of Deity*.
5. Paul Tillich, *Dynamics of Faith*, p. 45.
6. Don Cupitt, *Taking Leave of God*, p. 166.
7. Nietzsche, *Twilight of the Idols*, pp. 69f.
8. Bold type added.

Chapter 5
1. 2 Corinthians: 13:14.
2. Matthew 28:19.
3. Quoted by J.N.D. Kelly in *Early Christian Doctrines*, p. 89 (slightly adapted)

Chapter 6
1. John 1:14.
2. The recovery of the 'historical Jesus' will be discussed in the next chapter.
3. There is a wealth of material on this subject. As there is space here for only a short sketch, for much fuller treatment see the author's *Resurrection — A Symbol of Hope*.
4. 2 Kings 2:1–12.
5. Acts 7:55–56.
6. Jungian analysts document many contemporary accounts of how the unconscious mind can creatively resolve inner tensions by means of visions.
7. Mark 9:2–8.
8. This is reported by Josephus and narrated in a book "The Ascension of Moses".
9. Evans, *Resurrection and the New Testament*, p. 137.
10. Mark 16:6.
11. John 20:17.

12. See *Kerygma and Myth*, ed. by Hans Werner Bartsch, p. 41.
13. Romans 1:3–4. (Bold type added).
14. From John 1:1–9.
15. 2 Corinthians 12:1–7.
16. Mark 10:18.

Chapter 7

1. See Bibliography.
2. See chapter 3 of the author's *The World to Come*.
3. For a much fuller discussion of Hegel see the author's *Christian Faith at the Crossroads*, chapter 5.
4. Tillich, *Perspectives on Nineteenth and Twentieth Century Protestant Theology*, p. 115.
5. A fuller account is found in *Christian Faith at the Crossroads*, chapter 6.
6. See Chapter 9.
7. See Gordon Kaufman, *In Face of Mystery*.
8. Matthew 5:48.
9. Quoted by Hollingdale in *Nietzsche, the Man and His Philosophy*, p. 30.
10. Gore, ed., *Lux Mundi*, p. viii.
11. *Lux Mundi*, p. 155.
12. See Temple, *Nature, Man and God*, p. 478.
13. Altizer, *The Descent into Hell*, p. 40.

Chapter 8

1. See von Rad, *Wisdom in Israel*, p. 287.
2. Proverbs 10:1.
3. Proverbs 26:17–19.
4. G. von Rad, *Wisdom in Israel*, p. 317.
5. Ecclesiasticus 47:14–17.
6. See 1 Kings 3:5–14.
7. Proverbs 6:6–11.
8. Ecclesiasticus 11:14.
9. Proverbs 8:22–3. See also Proverbs 8:1–36, Ecclesiasticus 24:1–22, Wisdom 7:22–30, 9:9.
10. Wisdom 7:24–26.
11. Psalm 14:1.
12. James 1:27.
13. Jeremiah 31:30, Ezekiel 18.
14. Jeremiah 31:29, Ezekiel 18:2.
15. Proverbs 11:31.
16. Rubenstein, *After Auschwitz*, p. 238.
17. Daniel 12:3.
18. For a fuller discussion see the author's *Resurrection – A Symbol of Hope*.
19. Job 19:25. The original meaning of this verse has long been overlaid in the popular mind by the Christian interpretation, made famous because of its use in Handel's *Messiah*.

20. Ecclesiastes 3:10–11, 7:14.
21. Ecclesiastes 2:24; 3:13, 22; 5:18; 8:15; 9:7.
22. Ecclesiastes 12:11.
23. Witherington, *Jesus the Sage*, p. 57.
24. See especially Wisdom 9:1–11:14.
25. Wisdom 8:19–20, 9:15.
26. Wisdom 3:1–4.

Chapter 9

1. Matthew 5:17.
2. Hebrews 4:14.
3. Funk, *Honest to Jesus*, p. 302.
4. ibid.
5. Ecclesiastes 1:3.
6. Matthew 16:26.
7. Ecclesiastes 1:15.
8. Matthew 6:27.
9. Ecclesiastes 2:14.
10. Matthew 5:45.
11. Sirach 29:23.
12. Luke 10:7–8.
13. Sirach 13:15.
14. Matthew 5:46.
15. Proverbs 25:28.
16. Matthew 13:33.
17. Proverbs 22:16.
18. Luke 18:25.
19. Ecclesiastes 9:14–16.
20. Luke 18:2–5.
21. Matthew 7:1–2.
22. Sirach 18:20.
23. Matthew 6:19–20.
24. Sirach 29:10–11.
25. Wisdom 10:10.
26. Luke 18:25.
27. Matthew 7:3–5.
28. Matthew 5:40.
29. Ecclesiastes 2:24; 3:13, 22; 5:18; 8:15; 9:7.
30. Matthew 11:19.
31. Matthew 6:25–30.
32. Matthew 8:22.
33. John 10:10.
34. Luke 13:24.
35. Mark 2:27–28.
36. Matthew 5:44.
37. Matthew 5:46, 39, 41–42.

38. Luke 23:34. This was probably a very late insertion in the text for it does not appear in some of the most important manuscripts.
39. James 1:5.
40. James 3:13–17.
41. James 4:13–16.
42. The quotations from the Didache used here are from *Early Christian Writings*, Penguin Books, 1968.
43. Proverbs 3:17.
44. See Acts 9:2, 18:25, 19:23, 22:4, 24:14.
45. The issue is extensively discussed in the author's *Resurrection – A Symbol of Hope*.
46. 1 Corinthians 1:20–25.

Chapter 10

1. This is the first definition offered by the Shorter Oxford Dictionary.
2. Kaufman, *In Face of Mystery*, p. 347.
3. Don Cupitt used this phrase for the title of his book *Taking Leave of God*, having found it in a sermon by the mediaeval mystic Meister Eckhart: 'Man's last and highest parting occurs when, for God's sake, he takes leave of God'.
4. Matthew 23:4
5. John 8:32.
6. *Westminster Confession of Faith*, Chap. XXXI, article IV.
7. See 'A critique of traditional theistic religion' in the *South African Journal of Philosophy*, vol. 4, no. 2, 1985, pp. 55–61.
8. Prozesky's challenge to theism was later expounded in some detail in 'Implications of Apartheid for Christianity' in *Christianity Amidst Apartheid:Selected Perspectives on the Church in South Africa*, ed. by Martin Prozesky, 1990, Macmillan, London, pp. 122–46.
9. See I Kings 11:5, 33; II Kings 23:13.
10. I Corinthians 14:34.
11. Mary Daly, *Beyond God the Father*, p. 19.
12. Genesis 1:26.
13. 'The Genesis of Pollution', *Horizon* (New York: American Heritage), Summer 1973, p. 7.
14. See chapter 7 above.
15. Quoted by Harvey in *Feuerbach and the interpretation of religion*, p. 164.
16. *The New Religion of Life, The Meaning of it All, Kingdom Come*.
17. Acts 2:42.
18. Luke 17:20–21.
19. Luke 7:22.

Select Bibliography

Altizer, Thomas J. J. and William Hamilton, *Radical Theology and the Death of God*, Penguin Books, 1968

Altizer, Thomas J.J., *The Descent into Hell*, Seabury Press, 1979

Armstrong, Karen, *A History of God*, Heinemann, 1993

Bartsch, Hans Werner (Ed.), *Kerygma and Myth*, S.P.C.K., 1953

Cupitt, Don, *Taking Leave of God*, SCM Press, 1980

_____, *Creation out of Nothing*, SCM Press, 1990

_____, *After God, The Future of Religion*, BasicBooks, 1997

_____, *The New Religion of Life in Everyday Speech*, SCM Press, 1999

_____, *The Meaning of It All in Everyday Speech*, SCM Press, 1999.

_____, *Kingdom Come in Everyday Speech*, SCM Press, 2000

_____, *Reforming Christianity*, Polebridge Press, 2001

Daly, Mary, *Beyond God the Father*, Beacon Press, 1973

de Rosa, Peter, *Jesus Who Became Christ*, Collins, 1975

Dickie, John, *The Organism of Christian Truth*, James Clarke & Company, 1930

Edwards, David L., *The Futures of Christianity*, Hodder & Stoughton, 1987

Evans, C. F., *Resurrection and the New Testament*, SCM Press, 1970

Feuerbach, Ludwig, *The Essence of Christianity*, [1841], translated by George Eliot, Harper & Row, 1957

Freeman, Anthony, *God in Us, A Case for Christian Humanism*, SCM Press, 1993.

Funk, Robert W., *Honest to Jesus*, Polebridge Press, 1996

Geering, Lloyd, *Resurrection – A Symbol of Hope*, Hodder & Stoughton, 1971

_____, *New Idols for Old*, St. Andrew's Trust, Wellington, 1996.

_____, *The World to Come*, Polebridge Press, 1999

_____, *Tomorrow's God*, Polebridge Press, 2000.

_____, *Christian Faith at the Crossroads*, Polebridge Press, 2001

Gore, Charles, (ed.), *Lux Mundi*, John Murray, London, 1891

Hall, Douglas John, *The End of Christendom and the Future of Christianity*, Trinity Press International, 1997

Harnack, Adolf, *What is Christianity?* (1900), reprinted by Harper Torchbooks.

Hartshorne, M. Holmes, *The Faith to Doubt*, Prentice-Hall Inc., 1963

Harvey, Van A., *Feuerbach and the interpretation of religion*, Cambridge University Press, 1997

Hollingdale, R. J., *Nietzsche, the Man and his Philosophy*, Routledge & Kegan Paul, 1965

Hopper, Stanley Romaine, *The Crisis of Faith*, Hodder & Stoughton, 1947

James, E. O., *The Ancient Gods*, Weidenfeld & Nicolson, 1960

Kaufman, Gordon D., *In Face of Mystery*, Harvard University Press, 1993

Kee, Alistair, *The Roots of Christian Freedom*, SPCK, 1988

Kelly, J. N. D., *Early Christian Doctrines*, Adam & Charles Black, 1968

Kerr, H.T., (ed.), *A Compend of Luther's Theology*, Westminster Press, 1943

Kloppenborg, Verben, John S., *Excavating Q, The History and Setting of the Sayings Gospel*, Fortress Press, 2000

Macquarrie, John, *In Search of Deity*, SCM Press, 1984

Maringer, J., *The Gods of Prehistoric Man*, Weidenfeld & Nicolson, 1960

Marxsen, Willi, *The Resurrection of Jesus of Nazareth*, SCM Press, 1970

McFague, Sallie, *Super, Natural Christians*, Fortress Press, 1997

Nietzsche, Friedrich, *Twilight of the Idols and The Anti-Christ*, trans. By R.J. Hollingdale, Penguin Books, 1968

Otto, Rudolf, *The Idea of the Holy*, Oxford University Press, 1923

Rubenstein, Richard R., *After Auschwitz*, The Bobbs-Merrill Company, 1966

Smith, Wilfred Cantwell, *The Meaning and End of religion*, A Mentor Book, 1964

_____, *Belief and History*, University Press of Virginia, 1977

_____, *Faith and Belief*, Princeton University Press, 1979

_____, *Towards a World Theology*, Macmillan Press, 1981

Spong, John Shelby, *Why Christianity Must Change or Die*, HarperSanFrancisco, 1998

Temple, William, *Nature, Man and God*, Macmillan, 1964

Thrower, James, *A Short History of Western Atheism*, Pemberton Books, 1971

Tillich, Paul, *Dynamics of Faith*, George Allen & Unwin, 1957

_____, *Perspectives on Nineteenth and Twentieth Century Protestant Theology*, ed. by Carl E. Braaten, SCM Press, 1967

Toynbee Arnold, *Mankind and Mother Earth*, Oxford University Press, 1976

van de Pol, W. H., *The End of Conventional Christianity*, Newman Press, 1968

Vermes, Geza, *The Changing Faces of Jesus*, Penguin Books, 2001

Von Rad, Gerhard, *Wisdom in Israel*, SCM Press, 1972

Witherington, III, Ben, *Jesus the Sage*, Fortress Press, 1994

Wrede, William, *The Messianic Secret*, trans. by J. C. G. Greig, James Clarke & Co. Ltd., 1971

Index

155